LIFE OF DISOBEDIENCE
AND
LIFE OF OBEDIENCE
- THE TEN PLAGUES -

Dr. Jaerock Lee

> *"'For I know the plans that I have for you,'
> declares the LORD,
> 'plans for welfare and not for calamity
> to give you a future and a hope.'"*
>
> *(Jeremiah 29:11)*

LIFE OF DISOBEDIENCE AND LIFE OF OBEDIENCE
- THE TEN PLAGUES -
by Dr. Jaerock Lee

Published by Urim Books (Representative: Kyungtae Noh)
73, Yeouidaebang-ro 22-gil, Dongjak-Gu, Seoul, Korea
www.urimbooks.com

All rights reserved. This book or parts thereof may not be reproduced in any form, stored in a retrieval system, or transmitted in any form or by any means, electronic, mechanical, photocopying, recording or otherwise, without prior written permission of the publisher

Unless otherwise noted, all Scripture quotations are taken from the Holy Bible, NEW AMERICAN STANDARD BIBLE, ®, Copyright © 1960, 1962, 1963, 1968, 1971, 1972, 1973, 1975, 1977, 1995 by The Lockman Foundation. Used by permission.

Copyright © 2008 by Dr. Jaerock Lee
ISBN: 978-89-7557-147-3, ISBN: 978-89-7557-060-5(set)
Translated by Dr. Esther K. Chung. Used by permission.

Previously published in Korean by Urim Books, Seoul, Korea.
Copyright © 2007 by Dr. Jaerock Lee

First Edition April 2008
Second Edition August 2009

Edited by Dr. Geumsun Vin
Designed by Editorial Bureau of Urim Books
For more information contact at urimbook@hotmail.com

Prologue

The Civil War in the United States reached the peak when the sixteenth president, Abraham Lincoln, proclaimed a day of fasting prayer on April 30, 1863.

"Today's fearful disasters may be the punishment for the sins of our fathers. We were too proud of our success and wealth. We were so proud that we forgot to pray to God who created us. We have to confess the sins of our nation and ask for God's mercy and grace with humble attitude. This is the duty of the citizens of the United States of America."

As the great leader suggested, many Americans did not eat for a day and offered up fasting prayer.

Lincoln humbly prayed to God and saved the United States of America from falling apart. In fact, we can find all the answers to problems in God.

The gospel has been preached by many preachers

throughout the centuries, but many people do not listen to the word of God, saying they'd rather believe in themselves.

Today, there are unusual temperature changes and natural disasters happening around the world. Even with the development in medicines, there are new and treatment-resistant diseases that are becoming more virulent.

People may have confidence in themselves. People may distance themselves from God, but when we look at the inside of their lives, we cannot talk about it without mentioning the words like anxiety, pain, poverty, and disease.

In one day a person can lose his health. Some people lose their dear family members or lose all their fortune due to accidents. Others may have many difficulties in their businesses and workplaces.

They may cry out, "Why do these things have to happen to me?" But, they do not know the way out. Even many believers suffer from trials and tests and don't know the way out.

But, everything has its cause. All problems and difficulties also have causes.

The Ten Plagues inflicted upon Egypt, and the rules for the Passover recorded in the Book of Exodus give the clue of solutions to all kinds of problems with which all mankind meet on the face of the earth today.

Egypt spiritually refers to the world, and the lesson from the Ten Plagues on Egypt is applied to everybody around the globe even today. But not many people realize the will of God contained in the Ten Plagues.

Since the Bible does not say that it is the 'Ten Plagues,' some people say that it is eleven or even twelve plagues.

The former opinion includes the case of turning the staff of Aaron into a snake. But there isn't really any damage caused by seeing a snake, so it is, in a sense, difficult to include it as one of the plagues.

But because a snake in wilderness has very strong poison to kill any person with one bite, one may feel very threatened just seeing a snake. That is why some people include it as one of the plagues.

The latter opinion includes the incident of the staff turning into a snake and also the Egyptian soldiers' death in the Red

Sea. Since the people of Israel had not yet crossed the Red Sea at that moment, they include this incident and say there were twelve plagues. But the important thing is not the number of plagues but the spiritual meaning and the providence of God contained in them.

In this book are portrayed, in contrast, the life of Pharaoh, who disobeyed the word of God, and the life of Moses who led a life of obedience. It also contains the love of God who with His limitless compassion lets us know the way of salvation through the celebration of Passover, the law of circumcision, and the meaning of the Feast of Unleavened Bread.

Pharaoh witnessed the power of God but still disobeyed Him, and he fell into an irreversible state. But the Israelites were safe from all disasters because they obeyed.

The reason why God tells us about the Ten Plagues is to let us realize why tests and trials come upon us, so that we can solve all the problems of life and lead a life free of any disaster. Furthermore, by telling us about the blessings that will come upon us when we obey, He wants us to possess the heavenly kingdom as His children.

Those who read this book will be able to find the keys to solving the problems of life. They will feel the quenching of spirit like they taste sweet rain after a long drought, and be guided to the way of answers and blessings.

I give thanks to Geumsun Vin, the director of editorial bureau and all workers who have made this publication possible. I pray in the name of the Lord Jesus Christ that all the readers will lead a life of obedience so that they will receive amazing love and blessings of God.

July 2007

Jaerock Lee

Table of Contents

On Life of Disobedience

Chapter 1
Ten Plagues Inflicted upon Egypt — 3

Chapter 2
Life of Disobedience and Plagues — 19

Chapter 3
Plagues of Blood, Frogs, and Gnats — 31

Chapter 4
Plagues of Flies, Pestilence, and Boils — 49

Chapter 5
Plagues of Hails and Locusts — 65

Chapter 6
Plagues of Darkness and Death of the Firstborn — 79

On Life of Obedience

Chapter 7
Passover and Way of Salvation   93

Chapter 8
Circumcision and Holy Communion   107

Chapter 9
Exodus and the Feast of Unleavened Bread   123

Chapter 10
Life of Obedience and Blessings   135

On Life of Disobedience

But it shall come about,
if you do not obey the LORD your God,
to observe to do all His commandments and
His statutes with which I charge you today,
that all these curses will come upon you and overtake you:
Cursed shall you be in the city,
and cursed shall you be in the country.
Cursed shall be your basket and your kneading bowl.
Cursed shall be the offspring of your body
and the produce of your ground,
the increase of your herd and the young of your flock.

Cursed shall you be when you come in,
and cursed shall you be when you go out
(Deuteronomy 28:15-19).

Chapter 1

Ten Plagues Inflicted upon Egypt

Exodus 7:1-7

Then the LORD said to Moses, "See, I make you as God to Pharaoh, and your brother Aaron shall be your prophet. You shall speak all that I command you, and your brother Aaron shall speak to Pharaoh that he let the sons of Israel go out of his land. But I will harden Pharaoh's heart that I may multiply My signs and My wonders in the land of Egypt. When Pharaoh does not listen to you, then I will lay My hand on Egypt and bring out My hosts, My people the sons of Israel, from the land of Egypt by great judgments. The Egyptians shall know that I am the LORD, when I stretch out My hand on Egypt and bring out the sons of Israel from their midst." So Moses and Aaron did it; as the LORD commanded them, thus they did. Moses was eighty years old and Aaron eighty-three, when they spoke to Pharaoh.

Everyone has a right to be happy, but not many people actually feel happy. Especially in today's world that is so full of various forms of accidents, diseases, and crimes it is difficult to guarantee anybody's happiness.

But there is somebody who wants us to experience happiness more than anybody else. It is our Father God who created us. In the heart of most parents is the desire to give everything to their children, unconditionally, for their happiness. Our God loves us far more than any parents and He wants to bless us far more than any parent's desire.

How could this God ever want His children to suffer anguish or experience disasters? Nothing could be further from God's desire for us.

If we are able to realize the spiritual meaning and the providence of God contained in the Ten Plagues inflicted on Egypt, we can understand that it was also His love. Furthermore, we can discover the ways to avoiding disasters. But even in the face of disaster we can find and be shown the way out and continue to go the way of blessings.

When faced with difficulties, many people do not believe in Him, but still complain against God. Even among believers there are some who do not understand the heart of God when they face hardships. They just lose heart and fall into despair.

Job was the richest man in the East. But when disasters came upon him, at first he didn't understand the will of God.

He spoke as though he expected that what had happened to him could come upon him. It is expressed in Job 2:10. He said that since he received blessings from God, there was a chance he could also receive misfortune as well. However, he misunderstood that God gives blessings and disasters without cause or reason.

The heart of God for us is never calamity but peace. Before we get into the Ten Plagues inflicted upon Egypt, let us think about the situation and circumstances at that time.

The Making of the Israelites

Israel is the chosen people of God. In their history, we can find the providence and will of God very well. Israel was the name given to Jacob, the grandson of Abraham. Israel means *"you have striven with God and with men and have prevailed"* (Genesis 32:28).

Isaac was born to Abraham, and Isaac had twin sons. They were Esau and Jacob. It was unusual that the second son, Jacob, held on to the heel of his brother Esau when they were born. Jacob wanted to take the right of the firstborn instead of his elder brother Esau.

That is why Jacob later bought the birthright from Esau with some bread and lentil stew. He also deceived his father,

Isaac, to take the blessings of the first son from Esau.

Today, people's minds have changed a lot, and people leave inheritance not only for sons but also for their daughters. But in the past, the first son usually received all the inheritance from their fathers. In Israel, too, this blessing for the first son was great.

The Bible tells us that Jacob took the blessings of the first son in a deceitful way, but he really longed to receive the blessings of God. Until he actually received blessings, he had to go through many kinds of difficulties. He had to flee from his brother. He served his uncle, Laban for twenty years and while serving him he bore with being frequently deceived and cheated by him.

When Jacob came back to his hometown, he was in a life-threatening situation because his brother was still angry with him. Jacob had to go through these difficulties because he had the cunning nature to seek his own advantage or benefit.

But because he feared God more than others, he destroyed his ego and 'self' through these times of trials. Thus, he finally received the blessing of God and the nation of Israel was formed through his twelve sons.

Background of Exodus and Appearance of Moses

Why did Israelites live as slaves in Egypt?

Jacob, the father of Israel, showed favoritism towards his eleventh son, Joseph. Joseph was born of Rachel, the wife that Jacob loved most dearly. This triggered the envy of Joseph's half-brothers, and finally, Joseph was sold into Egypt by his brothers as a slave.

Joseph feared God and acted with integrity. He walked with God in everything and in just thirteen years from the time he was sold to Egypt, he became the ruler after the king over all the lands of Egypt.

There was such a severe drought in the Near East, and with the favor of Joseph, Jacob and his family moved into Egypt. Because Egypt was saved from that severe drought through the wisdom of Joseph, the Pharaoh and the Egyptians treated his family extremely well and gave over the land in Goshen to them.

After many generations passed, the Israelites prevailed in number. The Egyptians felt threatened. Because it was hundreds of years since Joseph had died, they had already forgotten the grace of Joseph.

After all, the Egyptians began to persecute the Israelites and made them slaves. The Israelites were forced to do harsh labor.

Moreover, to stop the growing number of Israelites, the Pharaoh commanded the Hebrew midwives to kill all the newborn boys.

Moses, the leader of the Exodus, was born in this dark era. His mother saw that he was beautiful and hid him for three months. The time when she could hide him no longer came, and she put him in a wicker basket and set it among the reeds by the bank of the Nile.

At that time, the princess of Egypt came down to bathe at the Nile. She saw the basket and wanted to take and keep the baby. Moses' sister had been observing what had happened and she quickly recommended Jochebed, the real mother of Moses, as a mid-wife. This way, Moses was raised by his own mother.

Naturally, he came to learn about the God of Abraham, Isaac, and Jacob, and about the Israelites.

Growing in the palace of Pharaoh, Moses acquired various kinds of knowledge that would prepare and equip him as a leader. At the same time he learned clearly about his people and God. His love for both God and for his people also grew up.

God chose Moses as the leader of the Exodus and from birth he learned and practiced leadership and control.

Moses, Man of God, and the Pharaoh

One day, there was a turning point in Moses' life. He had always worried about his people, the Hebrews, and he had anxiety over their toil and suffering as slaves. One day, he saw an Egyptian beating a Hebrew man. He couldn't hold his anger and killed the Egyptian. Eventually the Pharaoh heard about it and Moses had to flee from him.

Moses was to spend the next forty years as a shepherd tending sheep in the Midian wilderness. All this was in the providence of God to prepare him as the leader of the Exodus. During the forty years shepherding the sheep of his father-in-law in the wilderness, he completely forsook the dignity as a prince of Egypt and became a very humble man.

It was only after all this that God called Moses as the leader of the Exodus.

> *But Moses said to God, "Who am I, that I should go to Pharaoh, and that I should bring the sons of Israel out of Egypt?" (Exodus 3:11)*

Since Moses had been only shepherding sheep for forty years, he had no confidence. God also knew his heart, and He Himself showed him many signs such as turning a staff into snake to let him go to Pharaoh and deliver the command of God.

Moses humbled himself completely and was able to obey the command of God. But the Pharaoh unlike Moses was a very stubborn man with a hardened heart.

A man with a hardened heart does not change even after seeing many works of God. In the well-known parable that Jesus told in Matthew 13:18-23, among the four kinds of fields, a hardened heart falls under the category of the 'roadside.' The roadside is very hard because people walk on it. Those who have this kind of heart do not change at all even after seeing the works of God.

At that time the Egyptians had very strong and brave character like lions. Their ruler, the Pharaoh, had the absolute power and considered himself to be a god. The people also served him as though he was a god.

Moses talked about God to the people who had this kind of cultural understanding. They knew nothing about the God of whom Moses spoke, and who was ordering the Pharaoh to let the Israelites go. It was obviously difficult for them to listen to Moses.

They were enjoying great benefit through the labor of Israelites, so it was even more difficult to accept it.

Today also, there are people who only consider their knowledge, fame, authority, or wealth the best. They seek only their own benefit and trust only in their own abilities. They are arrogant and their hearts are hardened.

Pharaoh and the Egyptians' hearts were hardened. So they did not obey the will of God delivered by Moses. They disobeyed until the end, and finally, they were put to death.

Of course, even though Pharaoh's heart was hardened, God did not allow great plagues from the beginning.

As said, *"The LORD is gracious and merciful; slow to anger and great in lovingkindness"* (Psalm 145:8), God showed them His power through Moses many times. God wanted them to acknowledge Him and obey Him. But the Pharaoh hardened his heart even more.

God, who sees the heart and mind of every person, told Moses and let him know everything that He was going to do.

> But I will harden Pharaoh's heart that I may multiply My signs and My wonders in the land of Egypt. When Pharaoh does not listen to you, then I will lay My hand on Egypt and bring out My hosts, My people the sons of Israel, from the land of Egypt by great judgments. The Egyptians shall know that I am the LORD, when I stretch out My hand on Egypt and bring out the sons of Israel from their midst (Exodus 7:3-5).

Pharaoh's Hardened Heart and Ten Plagues

During the whole process of the Exodus, we can find many times the expression, "The LORD hardened Pharaoh's heart."

Literally, it seems that God hardened Pharaoh's heart purposely, and one may misunderstand that God is like a dictator. But it's not true.

God wants everyone to reach salvation (1 Timothy 2:4). He wants a man even with the most hardened heart to realize the truth and reach salvation.

God is the God of love; He would never purposely harden Pharaoh's heart in order to reveal His glory. Also, through the fact that God repeatedly sent Moses to the Pharaoh, we can understand that God wants the Pharaoh and everyone else to change their hearts and obey Him.

God does everything in order, in love, and within justice, following the word in the Bible.

If we do evil and not listen to the word of God, the enemy devil will accuse us. That is why we face tests and trials. Those who obey the word of God and live in righteousness will receive blessings.

Men choose their actions with their own freewill. God does not designate who will receive blessings and who will not. Had God not been a God of love and justice, He could have inflicted a great plague on Egypt right from the beginning to make the Pharaoh submit.

God does not want 'forced obedience' coming out of fear. He wants men to open their hearts and obey Him with their free will.

First, He lets us know His will and He shows His power so that we can obey. But when we don't obey, He begins with minor calamities to allow us to gain some realization and causes us to find ourselves.

The almighty God knows the heart of men; He knows when evils are revealed and how we can cast off evils and how to receive the solutions to our problems.

Even today He guides us to the best way and implies the best method to let us come forth as holy children of God.

From time to time, He allows us tests and trials that we can overcome. It is the way for us to find evil in us and cast it off. As our soul is prosperous, He lets everything go well with us and gives us good health.

The Pharaoh did not throw away his evil, however, when it was disclosed. He hardened his heart and kept on disobeying the word of God. Because God knew this heart of Pharaoh, He let the hardened heart of Pharaoh be revealed through the plagues. This is why the Bible says, "The LORD hardened Pharaoh's heart."

'Having a hardened heart' generally means that one's character is picky and stubborn. But the hardened heart recorded in the Bible with regards to the Pharaoh is not only to disobey God's word with wickedness, but also to take a stand against God.

As mentioned earlier, Pharaoh lived a very self-oriented life, even to consider himself like a god. All people obeyed him, and he had nothing to fear. If he had good heart, he would have believed in God seeing the powerful works manifested through Moses, even though he had not known about God before.

For example, Nebuchadnezzar of Babylon who lived from 605 to 562 BC, had not known about God, but as he witnessed the power of God manifested through Daniel's three friends

Shadrach, Meshach and Abed-nego, he acknowledged God.

> *Nebuchadnezzar responded and said, "Blessed be the God of Shadrach, Meshach and Abed-nego, who has sent His angel and delivered His servants who put their trust in Him, violating the king's command, and yielded up their bodies so as not to serve or worship any god except their own God. Therefore I make a decree that any people, nation or tongue that speaks anything offensive against the God of Shadrach, Meshach and Abed-nego shall be torn limb from limb and their houses reduced to a rubbish heap, inasmuch as there is no other god who is able to deliver in this way" (Daniel 3:28-29).*

Shadrach, Meshach and Abed-nego went to a Gentile country as captives at their young age. But to obey the commandments of God they did not bow down before an idol. They were thrown into a fiery furnace. But they were not harmed, and not even a hair of them was singed. When Nebuchadnezzar witnessed this, he acknowledged the living God immediately.

He not only acknowledged the almighty God when he witnessed the work of God transcending beyond any human ability; He also gave glory to God before all his people.

The Pharaoh, however, did not acknowledge God even after seeing His powerful works. He hardened his heart even more.

Only after he suffered from not only one or two plagues but all ten plagues did he let the Israelites go.

But since his hardened heart was basically still unchanged, he regretted letting the Israelites go. He chased them with his army, and finally he and his army died in the Red Sea.

The Israelites Were Under the Protection of God

While the whole land of Egypt was inflicted by the plagues and although the Israelites were in the same Egypt, they did not suffer from any of the plagues. It was because God provided His special protection over the land of Goshen where Israelites were living.

If God protects us, we can also be safe even in great disasters and afflictions. Even if we get a disease or face difficulties, we can be healed and overcome them by the power of God.

It's not because they had faith and were made righteous that Israelites were protected. They were protected by the fact that they were the chosen people of God. Unlike the Egyptians, they sought God in their sufferings, and because they acknowledged Him, they could be under His protection.

In the same way, even if we still have some forms of evil, just by the fact that we have become God's children, we can be protected from the disasters that come upon unbelievers.

It's because we were forgiven of our sins by the blood of

Jesus Christ, and have become God's children; therefore, we are no longer children of the devil that brings trials and disasters on us.

Furthermore, as our faith grows, we come to keep the Lord's Day holy, cast off evil, and obey the word of God, and thus, we can receive God's love and blessings.

> *Now, Israel, what does the LORD your God require from you, but to fear the LORD your God, to walk in all His ways and love Him, and to serve the LORD your God with all your heart and with all your soul, and to keep the LORD's commandments and His statutes which I am commanding you today for your good? (Deuteronomy 10:13)*

Chapter 2

Life of Disobedience and Plagues

Exodus 7:8-13

Now the LORD spoke to Moses and Aaron, saying, "When Pharaoh speaks to you, saying, 'Work a miracle,' then you shall say to Aaron, 'Take your staff and throw it down before Pharaoh, that it may become a serpent.'" So Moses and Aaron came to Pharaoh, and thus they did just as the LORD had commanded; and Aaron threw his staff down before Pharaoh and his servants, and it became a serpent. Then Pharaoh also called for the wise men and the sorcerers, and they also, the magicians of Egypt, did the same with their secret arts. For each one threw down his staff and they turned into serpents. But Aaron's staff swallowed up their staffs. Yet Pharaoh's heart was hardened, and he did not listen to them, as the LORD had said.

Karl Marx rejected God. He founded communism on the basis of materialism. His theory resulted in numerous people leaving God. It seemed that the whole world would soon adopt communism. But communism collapsed within 100 years.

Just as in the fall of communism, Marx suffered from such things in his personal life as a state of mental insecurity and the early deaths of his children.

Friedrich W. Nietzsche, who said *God is dead*, influenced many people to stand against God. But soon, he became a mad man due to fear and he finally faced a tragic end.

We can see that those who stand against God and disobey His word suffer from difficulties that are like plagues and they live very miserable lives.

Differences between Plagues, Trials, Tests, and Tribulations

Whether believers or not, all people may face some kind of problems in their lives. It is because our lives are in God's providence of human cultivation designed to gain true children.

God gave us only good things. But since sin came into men because of Adam's sin, this world came under the control of the enemy devil and Satan. From that time on, people began to suffer from various difficulties and sorrows.

Because of hatred, anger, covetousness, arrogance, and

adulterous minds people came to commit sins. According to the seriousness of the sin, they came to suffer from all kinds of tests and trials that are brought on by the enemy devil and Satan.

When they face very difficult situations, people say that it is a disaster. Also, when believers face difficult things, they often use the terminology 'test,' 'tribulation,' or 'trial.'

The Bible also says, *"And not only this, but we also exult in our tribulations, knowing that tribulation brings about perseverance; and perseverance, proven character; and proven character, hope"* (Romans 5:3-4).

According to whether or not each one lives by the truth, and according to how much measure of faith each one has, they can be called disasters or plagues, tests or tribulations.

For example, when a man has faith but does not act by the word that he has listened all the time, God cannot protect him from suffering many kinds of difficulties. This can be called a 'tribulation.' Furthermore, if he forsakes his faith and acts in untruth, he will suffer from plagues or disasters.

Also, suppose a person is listening to the word and trying to practice it, but does not completely live by the word completely right now. Then, he must have the process of struggling against his sinful natures. When a man meets with many kinds of difficulties for him to struggle against his sins to the point of shedding blood, the Bible says that he suffers trials or is disciplined. Namely, many kinds of difficulties that he meets with are called 'trials.'

Also, a 'test' is an occasion to check how much one's faith has grown. Thus, to those who try to live by the word, there are trials and tests that follow. If a person departs from the truth and enrages God, he will suffer from a 'tribulation' or 'plague.'

Causes of Plagues

When a person deliberately commits sins, God has to turn His face away from him. Then, the enemy devil and Satan can bring plagues upon him. Plagues come to the extent that one disobeys the word of God.

If he does not turn back but keeps on sinning even after he suffers from plagues, he will suffer from greater plagues like in the case of the Ten Plagues in Egypt. But if he repents and turns back, the plagues will go away soon by the mercy of God.

People suffer from plagues because of their evil, but we can find two groups of people among those who are suffering.

One group comes to God and tries to repent and turn back through the plagues. On the other hand, the other group still complains before God saying, "I diligently attend church, pray and give offerings, and why should I suffer from such a plague?"

The results will be completely different from each other. In the former case, the plague will be taken away and God's mercy will fall upon them. But in the latter, they don't even realize the problem, so greater plagues will come on them.

To the extent that a man has evil in his heart, it is difficult for him to recognize his fault and turn back. Such a person has such a hardened heart that he does not open the door of his heart even after hearing the gospel. Even if he has come into faith, he fails to understand the word of God; he just attends church but does not change himself.

Therefore, if you are suffering from a plague, you should realize that there was something improper in the sight of God, and quickly turn away and get away from the plague.

Chances Given by God

The Pharaoh rejected the word of God delivered to him through Moses. He did not turn away when minor plagues were inflicted, so he had to suffer from greater plagues. When he still kept on doing evil, not obeying God, his whole country became too weak to be able to recover. He finally died a tragic death. How foolish he was!

> *And afterward Moses and Aaron came and said to Pharaoh, "Thus says the LORD, the God of Israel, 'Let My people go that they may celebrate a feast to Me in the wilderness'" (Exodus 5:1).*

When Moses asked Pharaoh to send out the Israelites according to the word of God, Pharaoh refused immediately.

> *But Pharaoh said, "Who is the LORD that I should obey His voice to let Israel go? I do not know the LORD, and besides, I will not let Israel go" (Exodus 5:2).*

> *The God of the Hebrews has met with us. Please, let us go a three days' journey into the wilderness that we may sacrifice to the LORD our God, otherwise He will fall upon us with pestilence or with the sword (Exodus 5:3).*

When Pharaoh heard the word from Moses and Aaron, he unreasonably accused the people of Israel of being lazy and thinking about something other than their work. He persecuted them with a higher degree of cruel labor. The Israelites had previously been given straw to make bricks, but now they had to make the same number of bricks without being given the straw. It was not easy for the Israelites to make the number of bricks they had to even with the straw, but now the Pharaoh stopped giving them straw. We can see how hardened a heart Pharaoh had.

As their hard labor became heavier, Israelites began to complain against Moses. But God sent Moses to Pharaoh again to show the signs. God was giving Pharaoh, who was disobeying the word of God, a chance to repent by showing him God's power.

> *So Moses and Aaron came to Pharaoh, and thus they did just as the LORD had commanded; and Aaron threw his staff down before Pharaoh and his servants, and it became a serpent (Exodus 7:10).*

Through Moses, God made a serpent with a staff, to testify to the living God to Pharaoh who had not known God.

Spiritually, 'serpent' refers to Satan, and why did God made a serpent with the staff?

The land on which Moses was standing and the staff also belonged to this world. This world belongs to the enemy devil and Satan. To symbolize this fact, God made a serpent. It is to tell us that those who are not right in God's sight are always receiving the works of Satan.

Pharaoh stood against God, and so, God could not bless him. That is why God made a serpent appear, it represented Satan. It was to foreshadow that there would be works of Satan. The following plagues such as plagues of blood, frogs, and gnats were all done by the works of Satan.

Therefore, a staff turning into a serpent is a level where some little things take place so that a sensitive man may feel it. They may even be attributed as some coincidence. It is a stage where there is no actual damage. It is a chance given by God for one's repentance.

Pharaoh Brings in the Magicians of Egypt

As Pharaoh saw Aaron's staff turning into a serpent, Pharaoh called the wise men and sorcerers of Egypt.

They were magicians in the palace and did many tricks of magic before the king for entertainment. They went up to the positions of officials through the magic. Also, because it had been inherited from their ancestors, they were actually born with that kind of temperament.

Even today, some magicians pass through the Great Wall of China in front of so many people, or make the Statue of Liberty disappear. Also, some people have trained themselves with Yoga for a long time and thus they can sleep on a thin branch, or stay in a bucket for many days.

Some of these magic works are just deceptions of the eyes. Nonetheless, they train themselves to do some amazing things. Then, how much more powerful the sorcerers must have been since they were performing before the king for many generations! Especially, in their case, they could develop themselves to have contact with evil spirits.

Some sorceresses in Korea have contacts with demons, and they dance on a very sharp blades of grass cutters and not get hurt at all. The sorcerers of Pharaoh also had contacts with evil spirits and showed many kinds of amazing things.

The sorcerers in Egypt had been training themselves for a long period of time, and through illusion and trickery, they threw a staff and made it appear as a serpent.

Those Who Do Not Acknowledge the Living God

When Moses threw his staff and made a serpent, Pharaoh momentarily thought that there is God and the God of Israel is the true God. But when he saw the sorcerers make a serpent, he did not believe in God.

The serpents made by the sorcerers were eaten by the serpent made from the staff of Aaron, but he just thought it was coincidence.

In faith, there is no coincidence. But in case of a new believer who has just accepted the Lord, there may be many works of Satan to disturb him from believing in God. Then, many people just think of them as some kind of coincidence.

Also, some believers who have just accepted the Lord receive the solutions to their problems with the help of God. At first, they recognize the power of God, but as time goes, they just think it was coincidence.

Just as the Pharaoh witnessed the work of God turning a staff into a serpent, but did not recognize God, there are people who do not acknowledge the living God but just consider everything to be a coincidence even after experiencing the works of God.

Some people believe in God completely just by experiencing

God's work once. Some others at first acknowledge God but later, they think the problems were solved by their own ability, knowledge, experience, or through the help of the neighbors, and regard God's work as coincidence.

Thus, God cannot but turn His face away from them. Consequently, the problem that had once been resolved may come again.

In case of a disease that was healed, it may reoccur, or it may even become more serious. In case of a problem in business, greater problems may rise than before.

When we regard God's answer just as coincidence, it will lead us to stay farther from God. Then, the same problem may come again or we may fall into even more difficult situations.

In the same way, because the Pharaoh considered work of God just as coincidence, he now began to suffer from real plagues.

"Yet Pharaoh's heart was hardened, and he did not listen to them, as the LORD had said" (Exodus 7:13).

Chapter 3

Plagues of Blood, Frogs, and Gnats

Exodus 7:20-8:19

So Moses and Aaron did even as the LORD had commanded. And he lifted up the staff and struck the water that was in the Nile, in the sight of Pharaoh and in the sight of his servants, and all the water that was in the Nile was turned to blood (7:20).

Then the LORD said to Moses, "Say to Aaron, 'Stretch out your hand with your staff over the rivers, over the streams and over the pools, and make frogs come up on the land of Egypt.'" So Aaron stretched out his hand over the waters of Egypt, and the frogs came up and covered the land of Egypt (8:5-6).

Then the LORD said to Moses, "Say to Aaron, 'Stretch out your staff and strike the dust of the earth, that it may become gnats through all the land of Egypt.'" They did so; and Aaron stretched out his hand with his staff, and struck the dust of the earth, and there were gnats on man and beast. All the dust of the earth became gnats through all the land of Egypt (8:16-17).

Then the magicians said to Pharaoh, "This is the finger of God." But Pharaoh's heart was hardened, and he did not listen to them, as the LORD had said (8:19).

God told Moses that Pharaoh's heart would be hardened, and he would refuse to let the Israelites go even after seeing the staff turning into a serpent. Then, God told Moses what to do in detail.

> *Go to Pharaoh in the morning as he is going out to the water, and station yourself to meet him on the bank of the Nile; and you shall take in your hand the staff that was turned into a serpent (Exodus 7:15).*

Moses encountered Pharaoh who was walking by the Nile. Moses delivered the word of God holding the staff that had turned into serpent in his hand.

> *You shall say to [Pharaoh], "The LORD, the God of the Hebrews, sent me to you, saying, 'Let My people go, that they may serve Me in the wilderness. But behold, you have not listened until now.' Thus says the LORD, 'By this you shall know that I am the LORD: behold, I will strike the water that is in the Nile with the staff that is in my hand, and it will be turned to blood. The fish that are in the Nile will die, and the Nile will become foul, and the Egyptians will find difficulty in drinking water from the Nile'" (Exodus 7:16-18).*

Plague of Blood

Water is something that is closest to us and is directly related with our life. Seventy percent of the human body consists of water; it is absolutely an essential thing for all living things.

Today, in the face of increasing world population and economic development, many countries are suffering from lack of water. The UN has enacted the 'World Water Day' to remind the countries of the importance of water. It is to encourage the people to make efficient use of the limited water resources.

In ancient China, they had a water-control minister. We can easily see water around us everywhere, but sometimes we fail to see how great its relative importance is in our lives.

What a great problem it would be if all the water in the country turned into blood! Pharaoh and Egyptians encountered such an amazing thing. The Nile turned into blood.

But Pharaoh hardened his heart and did not listen to God's word, for he had seen his sorcerers turning water into blood, too.

Moses showed him the living God, but Pharaoh just considered it as coincidence and denied it. Thus, to the extent that he had evil, a plague came upon him.

Moses and Aaron did just as the LORD had commanded. In the sight of Pharaoh and in the sight of his servants Moses lifted up the staff and struck the water that was in the Nile and all the water that was in the Nile was turned to blood.

Then, the Egyptians had to dig around the Nile to get drinking water. This was the first plague.

Spiritual Meaning of the Plague of Blood

Now, what is the spiritual meaning contained in the plague of blood?

The greater part of Egypt is desert and wilderness. Therefore, Pharaoh and his people had to suffer to a great extent since their drinking water changed into blood.

Not only had the drinking water and water for daily living turned bad, but also the fish in the water died, and there was foul smell. The discomfort was great.

In this sense, the plague of blood spiritually refers to the sufferings caused by things that are directly related to our daily life. They are the things that are irritating and painful, coming from the closest people around us such as family members, friends, and colleagues.

With regard to our Christian life, this plague can be something like persecutions or tests coming from our closest friends, parents, relatives, or neighbors. Of course, those with greater measures of faith will overcome them more easily, but those with little faith will suffer great pain due to the persecutions and tests.

Trials Coming upon Those Who Have Evil

There are two categories when we face trials.

First is the trial that comes when we do not live by the word of God. At this time, if we quickly repent and turn away, God will take the trial away.

James 1:13-14 says, *"Let no one say when he is tempted, 'I am being tempted by God'; for God cannot be tempted by evil, and He Himself does not tempt anyone. But each one is tempted when he is carried away and enticed by his own lust."*

The reason why we face difficulties is because we are drawn by our desires and do not live by the word of God, and thenceforth the enemy devil brings trials upon us.

Secondly, sometimes we try to be faithful in our Christian life, but still face some trials. It is the disturbing works of Satan that tries to make us forsake our faith.

If we compromise in this case, the difficulties will become greater, and we will not be able to receive blessings. Some people lose the little faith they had and go back to the world.

Anyway, both cases are caused because we have evil in us. Thus, we have to diligently find out the evil forms in us and turn away from them. We have to pray with faith and give thanks. Then, we can overcome the trials.

Just as Moses' serpent swallowed up the serpents of the

sorcerers, the world of Satan is also under the control of God. When God first called Moses, He showed a sign of changing a staff into a serpent and turning it back to a staff again (Exodus 4:4). This symbolizes the fact that even if a test comes upon us through the works of Satan, if we show our faith by relying on God completely, God will recover everything back to normal.

On the contrary, if we compromise, it is not faith, and we cannot experience God's works. If we are faced with a trial, we should rely on God completely and see the work of God taking the trial away with His power.

Everything is under the control of God. Thus, whether it is small or big, in any kind of test, if we rely on God completely and obey the word of God, the trial will not matter to us. God Himself will solve the problem and lead us to prosperity in everything.

But the important thing is that, if it is a minor plague, we can recover easily, but in case of a major plague, it is not easy to recover fully. Therefore, we have to always check ourselves with the word of truth, cast off evil forms, and live by the word of God, so that we will not face any plagues.

Tests for Men of Faith Are for the Purpose of Blessing

Sometimes, there are exceptional cases. Even those with great faith may encounter tests. The apostle Paul, Abraham,

Daniel and his three friends, and Jeremiah all suffered tests. Even Jesus was tempted by the devil three times.

Likewise, the tests that come upon those who have faith are for blessings. If they rejoice, give thanks and rely on God completely, the tests will turn into blessings and they can give glory to God.

Thus, it is possible for those who have faith to encounter tests because they can receive blessings through overcoming them. However, they will never be faced with a plague. Plagues come upon a person who commits mistakes and errors in the sight of God.

For example, the apostle Paul was persecuted so much for the Lord, but through the persecution he received greater power and played the crucial role in evangelizing the Roman Empire as the apostle for the Gentiles.

Daniel did not compromise with the schemes made by the evil people who were jealous of him. He did not stop praying, but only walked righteously. Finally, he was thrown into the lion's den, but he was not harmed at all. He glorified God greatly.

Jeremiah mourned and warned the people with tears when his people were committing sins before God. For this he was beaten and jailed. But even in a situation where Jerusalem was conquered by Nebuchadnezzar of Babylon and so many people were killed and taken as captives, Jeremiah was saved and well treated by that king.

With faith, Abraham passed the test of offering his son, Isaac, so that he could be called the friend of God. He received such great blessings in spirit and body that even the king of a nation received him with honors.

As explained, in most cases, trials come upon us because of the forms of evil we have, but there are also exceptional cases where men of God receive tests in their faith. But the result of this is blessing.

Plague of Frogs

Even after seven days from the time the Nile turned into blood, Pharaoh hardened his heart. Since his sorcerers also turned water into blood, he refused to let the people of Israel go.

As the king of a nation, Pharaoh had to care for the discomfort of his people who were suffering from lack of water, but he didn't really care about it, because his heart was hardened.

Because of this hardened heart of Pharaoh, the second plague was inflicted on Egypt.

> *The Nile will swarm with frogs, which will come up and go into your house and into your bedroom and on your bed, and into the houses of your servants and on your people, and into your ovens and into your kneading*

bowls. So the frogs will come up on you and your people and all your servants (Exodus 8:3-4).

As God told Moses, when Aaron stretched out his hand with his staff over the waters of Egypt, untold numbers of frogs began to cover the land of Egypt. Then, the magicians did the same with their secret arts.

Except in Antartica, there are more than 400 different kinds of frogs worldwide. Their sizes vary from 2.5 cm to 30 cm.

Some people eat frogs, but usually people are surprised or feel disgusted at the sight of frogs. Frog eyes pop out and they don't have a tail. Their hind legs have webbed feet and their skin is always wet. All these things cause some kind of uncomfortable feelings.

Not just a couple of them, but countless frogs covered the whole country. They sat on dining tables and jumped around in the bedrooms and on the beds. They couldn't even think of enjoying a meal or resting well and peacefully.

Spiritual Meaning of the Plague of Frogs

Then, what is the spiritual meaning contained in the plague of frogs?

The Book of Revelation 16:13 has an expression, "three unclean spirits like frogs." Frogs are one of the detestable animals, and spiritually, it refers to Satan.

The frogs going into the palace of the king and to the houses of the ministers and peoples means that this plague was inflicted upon everybody in the same way, regardless of their social positions.

Also, the frogs going up to and on the beds meant that there would be problems between the husbands and wives.

For example, suppose the wife is a believer but her husband is not, and the husband is having an affair. Then, when he is caught, he gives such an excuse as, "It's because you are attending church all the time."

If the wife believes her husband, who is blaming the church for their personal problems, and stays away from God, then this is a problem caused by 'Satan in the bedroom.'

People face this kind of plague because they have forms of evil. They seem to be leading a good life in faith, but as they are faced with tests, their hearts are shaken. Their faith and hope for heaven disappear. Their joy and peace disappear too, and they fear looking at the reality of the situation.

But if they truly have hope for heaven and love for God, and if they have true faith, they will not suffer because of difficulties that they go through on this earth. They will rather overcome them and begin to receive blessings.

The frogs went into the ovens and kneading bowls. The kneading bowls refers to our daily bread, and the oven our workplace or business field. This as a whole means Satan works in people's families, workplaces, business fields, and even in the daily food, so every one will be put into difficult and stressful situations.

In this kind of situation, some people do not overcome the trial thinking, "These trials are coming to me because of faith in Jesus," and then they go back to the world. It is to depart from the way of salvation and eternal life.

But if they acknowledge the fact that the difficulties came upon them because of their lack of faith and forms of evil, and then they repent of it, Satan's disturbing works will go away, and God will help them overcome the difficulties.

If we truly have faith, no trial or plague will be a problem to us. Even if we may face a trial, if we rejoice, give thanks, and be on alert and pray, all problems can be solved.

> *Then Pharaoh called for Moses and Aaron and said, "Entreat the LORD that He remove the frogs from me and from my people; and I will let the people go, that they may sacrifice to the LORD" (Exodus 8:8).*

Pharaoh asked Moses and Aaron to remove the frogs that overran the whole country. Through Moses' prayer, the frogs died out from the houses, the courts, and fields.

The people piled them up in heaps, and the land became foul. Now they had a relief. But as Pharaoh saw the relief, he changed his mind. He had promised that he would send the people of Israel if the frogs were removed, but he just changed his mind.

> "But when Pharaoh saw that there was relief, he hardened his heart and did not listen to them, as the LORD had said" (Exodus 8:15).

'To harden his heart' means that Pharaoh was stubborn. Even after seeing a series of God's works, he didn't listen to Moses. As a result, another plague was inflicted.

Plague of Gnats

God told Moses in Exodus 8:16, *"Say to Aaron, 'Stretch out your staff and strike the dust of the earth, that it may become gnats through all the land of Egypt.'"*

When Moses and Aaron did what they were told, the dust of the earth became gnats through all the land of Egypt.

The magicians tried with their secret arts to bring forth gnats, but they could not. They finally realized it could not be done by any power of man and confessed to the king.

> *This is the finger of God (Exodus 8:19).*

Until now, the magicians could do similar things like changing a staff into a serpent, changing water into blood, and bringing forth frogs. But they could not do such things any more.

Finally, they also had to acknowledge the power of God manifested through Moses. But Pharaoh still hardened his heart and did not listen to Moses.

Spiritual Meaning of the Plague of Gnats

In Hebrew the term 'Kinim' is variously translated into 'lice, fleas, or gnats.' Such insects are generally small insects that live in unclean places. They stick to the body of man or animals and suck blood. It is usually found in the hairs, clothes, or furs of animals. There are more than 3,300 different kinds of gnats.

When they suck the blood from the human body, it is itchy. It may also cause secondary infection such as recurrent fever or eruptive typhus.

Today, in clean cities we cannot easily find gnats, but there were many such insects that live on the human body due to lack of hygiene.

Then, what is the plague of gnats specifically?

The dust of the earth changed into gnats. Dust is a very small thing which can be blown away by our breath. Its sizes vary from 3-4μm (micrometer) to 0.5 mm.

Just as an almost insignificant thing like dust becomes living gnats to suck blood and gives difficulty and suffering, the plague of gnats symbolizes the cases in which little things that have been under the surface like nothing, suddenly rise up and grows into big problems to give us sufferings and pain.

Usually, itching is relatively a lesser pain than the pains of other diseases, but it is very irritating. Also, as gnats live in unclean places, the plague of gnats will come to a place where there is a form of evil.

For example, a little bit of quarrelling between brothers or between husband and wife may develop into a big fight. When they talk about a small thing that had happened in the past, it may also develop into a big fight. This is also a plague of gnats.

When such forms of evil as envy and jealousy in heart grow up to become hatred, when one fails to hold his temper and gets angry at someone, when one's little lies develop into big lies in an effort to hide them, these are all examples of the plague of gnats.

If there is a latent form of evil in the heart, then the person has afflictions in his heart. He may feel that a Christian life is difficult. A minor illness may come upon him. These things are also plagues of gnats. If we suddenly have fever or cold, or if we have little quarrels and problems, we should quickly look back on ourselves and repent.

Now, what does it mean that the gnats were on animals? Animals are living things and at that time, the number of animals, along with land, was a measure to see how rich a person was. The king, ministers, and people had vineyards and were raising cattle.

Today, what are our possessions? Not only houses, land, business or our workplace but also family members belong to the category of our 'possessions.' And since animals are living things, it refers to the family members who are living together.

'Gnats being on men and animals' means that as little problems grow bigger, not only ourselves but also our family members suffer.

Such examples are cases where the children suffer because of the wrongdoings of their parents, or the husband is suffering because of the fault of his wife.

In Korea, many little children are suffering from atopic dermatitis. It first starts with little bit of itching, and it soon spreads to the whole body to cause discharges from eruptions of the skin and boils.

In a severe case, some children's skin cracks from their head to toe to give out discharge. As their skin is torn, it is covered by pus and blood.

The parents, when they see their children are in this kind of situation, become so heartbroken for the fact that they cannot really do anything for their children.

Also, when parents get angry, their little children sometimes get a sudden fever. In many cases, sicknesses of little children are caused by the wrongdoings of their parents.

In this situation, if the parents check their lives and repent of not fulfilling their duty properly, not having peace with others, and whatever was not right in the sight of God, the children will soon be healed.

We can see that it is also God's love to allow these things to take place. The plague of gnats comes upon us when we have forms of evil. Thus, we should not consider even the small things as coincidence, but discover the forms of evil in us, and quickly repent and turn away from them.

Chapter 4

Plagues of Flies, Pestilence, and Boils

Exodus 8:21-9:11

"Then the LORD did so. And there came great swarms of insects into the house of Pharaoh and the houses of his servants and the land was laid waste because of the swarms of insects in all the land of Egypt" (8:24).

"Behold, the hand of the LORD will come with a very severe pestilence on your livestock which are in the field, on the horses, on the donkeys, on the camels, on the herds, and on the flock. So the LORD did this thing on the next day, and all the livestock of Egypt died; but of the livestock of the sons of Israel, not one died" (9:3;6).

"So they took soot from a kiln, and stood before Pharaoh; and Moses threw it toward the sky, and it became boils breaking out with sores on man and beast. The magicians could not stand before Moses because of the boils, for the boils were on the magicians as well as on all the Egyptians" (9:10-11).

The Egyptian magicians acknowledged the power of God after seeing the plague of gnats. But Pharaoh still hardened his heart and did not listen to Moses. The power of God that had been manifested until this time was enough for him to believe God. But he just relied on his strength and authority and considered himself as a god, and he did not fear God.

The plagues continued, but he did not repent but only hardened his heart even more. Thus, the plagues became greater, too. Up to the point where they had the plague of gnats, they could recover immediately only if they turned back. But at this point it is becoming increasingly difficult for them to recover.

Plague of Flies

Moses went before Pharaoh early in the morning according to the word of God. He once again delivered the message of God to let the people of Israel go.

> Now the LORD said to Moses, "Rise early in the morning and present yourself before Pharaoh, as he comes out to the water, and say to him, 'Thus says the LORD, "Let My people go, that they may serve Me"'" (Exodus 8:20).

Nevertheless, Pharaoh did not listen to Moses. This caused

the plague of flies to come upon them, not only in the palace of Pharaoh and houses of the ministers, but also throughout the land of Egypt. The land was full of flies.

Flies are harmful. They transfer such diseases as typhoid, cholera, tuberculosis, and leprosy. The common housefly can breed anywhere, even on body wastes and garbage. They eat anything whether it is waste or food. Their digestion is fast and they excrete waste every five minutes.

Different kinds of pathogenic organisms may be left on people's foods or utensils and can enter into the human body. Their mouths and their feet are covered by liquids that also carry pathogenic organisms. They are one of the biggest causes of contagious diseases.

Today, we have many preventive measures and cure, and there are not many diseases transferred by flies. But long ago, if any contagious disease broke out, many people lost their lives. Also, apart from contagious diseases, if flies sit on the foods that we eat, it will be difficult to eat them for they will not be clean.

And not only one or two flies, but countless flies covered the whole land of Egypt. How painful it must have been for the people! They must have been afraid just by observing the scene around them.

The whole land of Egypt was harmed by the dreadful swarms of flies. This means that the rebellion not only of Pharaoh but also of all Egyptians stretched out over all the lands of Egypt.

But to make a clear distinction between the Israelites and the Egyptians, there were no flies sent to the land of Goshen where the Israelites were living.

Go, sacrifice to your God within the land (Exodus 8:25).

Before God gave the first plague, He commanded them to give sacrifice to Him in the wilderness, but the Pharaoh told them to sacrifice to God within the land of Egypt. Now, Moses refused that suggestion and told him the reason.

It is not right to do so, for we will sacrifice to the LORD our God what is an abomination to the Egyptians. If we sacrifice what is an abomination to the Egyptians before their eyes, will they not then stone us? (Exodus 8:26)

Moses continued to say that they would go into the wilderness for three days and just follow the command of God. Pharaoh replied and told him not to go too far and also pray for him, too.

Moses told Pharaoh that the flies would disappear the right next day, and asked him to be faithful about his word to let the people of Israel go.

But after the flies left by the prayer of Moses, Pharaoh changed his mind and did not send out the people of Israel.

Through this we can understand how deceitful and crafty he was. We also see why he had to continually face plagues.

Spiritual Meaning of the Plague of Flies

Just as flies come from unclean places and transfer contagious diseases, if the heart of a man is evil and unclean, he will speak out evil words, and causes various diseases or problems to come upon him. This is the plague of flies.

This kind of plague, when it comes, not only comes upon oneself but also upon his wife/her husband and the workplace.

Matthew 15:18-19 says, *"But the things that proceed out of the mouth come from the heart, and those defile the man. For out of the heart come evil thoughts, murders, adulteries, fornications, thefts, false witness, slanders."*

Whatever is in men's heart comes out through the lips. From good heart, good words come out, but from unclean hearts, unclean words will come out. If we have untruthfulness and cunningness, and hatred and anger, those kinds of words and deeds will come out.

Slandering, judging, condemning, and cursing all come from evil and unclean hearts. That is why Matthew 15:11 says, *"It is not what enters into the mouth that defiles the man, but what proceeds out of the mouth, this defiles the man."*

Even unbelievers say things like, "Words fall like seeds," or

"Once you spill the water, you cannot put it back."

You cannot just cancel out what you have said. Especially in the life of a Christian, the confession of the lips is very important. According to what kinds of words you say, whether they are positive or negative, it may have different results for you.

If we have common cold or simple contagious disease, this belongs to the category of the plague of gnats. So, if we repent immediately, we can recover. But from the case of plague of flies, we cannot recover immediately even if we repent. Since it is caused by greater evil than the case of the plague of gnats, we will have to face the retribution.

Therefore, if we are faced with the plague of flies, we have to look back and repent thoroughly of the evil words and things like that. Only after we repent can the problem be solved.

In the Bible we can find people who received the retribution for their evil words. It was the case for Michal, a daughter of King Saul and wife of King David. In 2 Samuel chapter 6, when the Ark of the LORD God was brought back to the city of David, David was so happy and danced before everybody.

The Ark of the LORD was a symbol of God's presence. It was taken by the Philistines during the time of the judges but was recovered. It could not stay in the tabernacle and temporarily stayed in Kiriath-jearim for about 70 years. After David took the throne, he was able to move the Ark to the tabernacle in Jerusalem. He was so overjoyed.

Not only David but all peoples of Israel rejoiced together and praised God. But Michal, who was supposed to rejoice together with her husband, just looked down on the King and despised him.

> *How the king of Israel distinguished himself today! He uncovered himself today in the eyes of his servants' maids as one of the foolish ones shamelessly uncovers himself!* (2 Samuel 6:20)

Then, what did David say?

> *It was before the LORD, who chose me above your father and above all his house, to appoint me ruler over the people of the LORD, over Israel; therefore I will celebrate before the LORD. I will be more lightly esteemed than this and will be humble in my own eyes, but with the maids of whom you have spoken, with them I will be distinguished* (2 Samuel 6:21-22).

For Michal spoke out such evil words, she had no child to the day of her death.

Likewise, people commit so many sins with their lips, but they do not even realize that their words are sins. Because of the iniquities on the lips, retributions of sins come upon their workplaces, businesses, and families, but they don't even realize why. God also tells us about the importance of words.

> *An evil man is ensnared by the transgression of his lips, but the righteous will escape from trouble. A man will be satisfied with good by the fruit of his words, and the deeds of a man's hands will return to him (Proverbs 12:13-14).*

> *From the fruit of a man's mouth he enjoys good, but the desire of the treacherous is violence. The one who guards his mouth preserves his life; the one who opens wide his lips comes to ruin (Proverbs 13:2-3).*

> *Death and life are in the power of the tongue, and those who love it will eat its fruit (Proverbs 18:21).*

We should realize what kinds of consequences the evil word from our lips causes, so that we will speak only positive words, good and beautiful words, words of righteousness and light, and confessions of faith.

Plague of Pestilence

Even after suffering from the plague of flies, Pharaoh still hardened his heart and refused to let the Israelites go. Then, God allowed the plague of pestilence to happen.

At this time too, God sent Moses before He let loose the plague. He sent Moses to deliver His will.

> *For if you refuse to let them go and continue to hold them, behold, the hand of the LORD will come with a very severe pestilence on your livestock which are in the field, on the horses, on the donkeys, on the camels, on the herds, and on the flocks. But the LORD will make a distinction between the livestock of Israel and the livestock of Egypt, so that nothing will die of all that belongs to the sons of Israel (Exodus 9:2-4).*

To let them realize that it was not a coincidence but a plague brought by the power of God, He set a definite time, saying, "Tomorrow the LORD will do this thing in the land." This way He kept on giving them chances to repent.

If he had acknowledged the power of God even a little bit, Pharaoh would have changed his mind and not suffered any more plagues.

But he did not change his mind. As a result, the pestilence came upon them, and livestock which were in the field—horses, donkeys, camels, the herds, and the flocks—died.

On the contrary, not one of the livestock of the Israelites died. God let them realize that God is living and fulfills His word. Pharaoh knew this fact very well, but he still hardened his heart and had not changed his thinking.

Spiritual Meaning of the Plague of Pestilence

Pestilence is any disease that spreads quickly and kills large numbers of people or animals. Now, all livestock in Egypt died, and we can imagine how much damage it was.

For example, the Black Death or Bubonic Plague, which prevailed in Europe in the fourteenth century, was actually an epidemic that happened to animals like squirrels and rats. But it was spread to the people through fleas causing so many deaths. Since it was so contagious and the medical science was not very much developed, it took so many people's lives.

The livestock like the herds of cattle and horses, and the flocks of sheep and goats were a great part of the wealth of the people. Thus, the livestock symbolizes the possessions of the Pharaoh, the ministers, and the people. Livestock are living things, and in today's sense, it refers to our family members, colleagues and friends who stay with us in our homes, workplaces, or businesses.

The cause of the pestilence on the livestock of Egypt was the wickedness of the Pharaoh. Hence, the spiritual meaning of the plague of pestilence is that diseases will come upon our family members if we accumulate evil and God turns His face away.

For example, when parents disobey God, their beloved children may get a disease that is difficult to cure. Or, because of the wickedness of the husband, his wife may become sick.

When this kind of plague comes upon us, not only we have to look back on ourselves but also the whole family members should repent together.

From Exodus 20:4 onward, it says that the retribution of idolatry will go down to three to four generations.

Of course, God of love will not just punish in all cases. If the children are good in heart, accept God and live in faith, they will not face any plagues caused by the sins of their parents.

But if the children accumulate more evil upon the evil they inherited from their parents, they will face the consequences of the sins. In many cases, those children who are born in families that worship idols so much are born with inherited disability or have mental disorders.

Some people have lucky-charms pasted on the walls of their houses. Some others worship idols of Buddha. Still others put their names in Buddhist Temples. In this kind of serious idolatry, even if they themselves may not suffer from the plague, their children will have problems.

Therefore, the parents should always stay in the truth so that their sins will not go down to their children. If any of the family members get a disease that is difficult to cure, they have to check whether it was not caused by their sins.

Plague of Boils

Pharaoh watched the deaths of the livestock of Egypt, and

sent somebody to check what was happening in the land of Goshen where Israelites were living. Unlike in all other lands of Egypt, none of the livestock died in Goshen.

Even after experiencing undeniable work of God, Pharaoh did not turn back.

> Pharaoh sent, and behold, there was not even one of the livestock of Israel dead. But the heart of Pharaoh was hardened, and he did not let the people go (Exodus 9:7).

Finally, God told Moses and Aaron to take for themselves handfuls of soot from a kiln, and let Moses throw it toward the sky in the sight of Pharaoh. As they did what God told them, it became boils breaking out with sores on man and beast.

A boil is a localized swelling and inflammation of the skin resulting from infection of a hair follicle and adjacent tissue, having a hard central core, and forming pus.

In a serious case, one may have to have surgery. Some of the boils are bigger than 10cm in diameter. It swells and causes high fever and fatigue, and some people cannot even walk well. It is such a painful thing.

This boil was on men and animals, and even the magicians could not stand before Moses because of the boils.

In the case of the pestilence, only the livestock died. But in the case of the boils, not only the animals but also people had to suffer.

Spiritual Meaning of the Plague of Boils

Pestilence is internal disease, but the boil is seen on the outside when something inside has become more serious.

For example, a small cancer cell grows up and then finally, it shows on the outside. It's the same with cerebral apoplexy or paralysis, lung diseases, and AIDS.

These diseases are usually found in those people who have stubborn characters. It may be different in each case, but many of them are very short-tempered, arrogant, do not forgive others and think they themselves are the best. Also, they insist on their opinions only and ignore others. It's all because of a lack of love. The plagues come due to these reasons.

Sometimes, we may wonder, "He looks very gentle and good, and why is he suffering from such a disease?" But even though one may look gentle on the outside, he may not be really so in the sight of God.

If he himself is not stubborn, it is probably because of the great sins committed by his forefathers (Exodus 20:5).

When the plague comes because of a family member, the problem will be solved when all of the family members repent together. Through this, if they become a peaceful and beautiful family, it becomes a blessing for them.

God controls the life, death, fortune, and misfortune of men within His justice. So, no plague or disaster comes without reason (Deuteronomy 28).

Also, even when the children are suffering because of the sins of their parents or ancestors, the fundamental cause is with the children themselves. Even if the parents worship idols, if the children live in the word of God, God protects them, so plagues will not come upon them.

The retribution for the sins of ancestral idolatry or that of parents comes down to the children because the children themselves do not live by the word of God. If they live in the truth, the God of justice protects them, so there won't be any problems.

Because God is love, He considers one soul more precious than the whole world. He wants every single person to reach salvation, live in the truth, and win the victory in his life.

God allows us plagues not to drive us to destruction but to lead us to repent of our sins and turn away from them according to His love.

The plagues of blood, frogs, and gnats are caused by the works of Satan, and they are relatively weak. So, if we repent and turn away, they can be resolved easily.

But the plagues of flies, pestilence, and boils are more serious, and they directly touch our bodies. Thus, in these cases, we have to tear our heart and repent very thoroughly.

If we are suffering from any of these plagues, we should not blame any other person. We have to be wise enought to reflect ourselves on the word of God and repent whatever was not right in the sight of God.

Chapter 5

Plagues of Hails and Locusts

Exodus 9:23-10:20

Moses stretched out his staff toward the sky, and the LORD sent thunder and hail, and fire ran down to the earth. And the LORD rained hail on the land of Egypt. So there was hail, and fire flashing continually in the midst of the hail, very severe, such as had not been in all the land of Egypt since it became a nation (9:23-24).

So Moses stretched out his staff over the land of Egypt, and the LORD directed an east wind on the land all that day and all that night; and when it was morning, the east wind brought the locusts. The locusts came up over all the land of Egypt and settled in all the territory of Egypt; they were very numerous. There had never been so many locusts, nor would there be so many again (10:13-14).

Those parents who really love their children will not refuse to discipline or spank their children. It is the desire of the parents to guide their children into doing what is right.

When the children do not listen to the scolding of their parents, they sometimes have to use the rod so that the children will keep it in mind. But the pain in the parents' heart is greater than the physical pain of the children.

The God of love also sometimes turns His face away to allow a plague or problems so that His beloved children can repent and turn away from it.

Plague of Hail

God could have sent a great plague from the beginning to make the Pharaoh submit. But God is patient; He endures for a long time. He showed His power, and guided Pharaoh and his people to acknowledge God, beginning with a minor plague.

> *For if by now I had put forth My hand and struck you and your people with pestilence, you would then have been cut off from the earth. But, indeed, for this reason I have allowed you to remain, in order to show you My power and in order to proclaim My name through all the earth. Still you exalt yourself against My people by not letting them go. Behold, about this time tomorrow, I will send a very heavy hail, such as has not been seen*

in Egypt from the day it was founded until now (Exodus 9:15-18).

The plagues became bigger and bigger, but Pharaoh still exalted himself against Israelites by not letting them go. Now, God allowed the seventh plague, the plague of hail.

God let Pharaoh know through Moses that there would be such heavy hail as had not been seen in Egypt from the day it was founded. And God gave the chances so that the people and the animals in the fields could hide inside. He warned them beforehand that if any men or animals stayed outside, they would die because of the hail.

Some servants of Pharaoh feared the word of the LORD and made their servants and their livestock flee to take refuge in the houses. But many others still did not fear the word of God and did not care.

But he who paid no regard to the word of the LORD left his servants and his livestock in the field (Exodus 9:21).

The next day Moses stretched out his staff toward the sky, and God sent thunder and hail. Fire ran down to the earth. It surely should have devastated the men, animals, trees and the vegetables in the field. How great the plague was!

But Exodus 9:31-32 says, *"Now the flax and the barley were ruined, for the barley was in the ear and the flax was in bud.*

But the wheat and the spelt were not ruined, for they ripen late." So, the damage was partial.

All the lands of Egypt suffered great damage because of the hail with fire, but nothing like that occurred in the land of Goshen.

The Spiritual Meaning of the Plague of Hail

Normally, hail falls without prior notice. It doesn't usually fall on a large area but relatively small areas locally.

Thus, the plague of hail symbolizes some great things happening in one part, but not in all aspects.

There was hail with fire to kill men and animals. The vegetables in the fields were damaged, and there was no food. This is a case of having a great damage to one's wealth due to unexpected accidents.

One may face a great loss due to fire in his workplace or business. One's family members may have a disease or get into an accident and it may cost a fortune to take care of it.

For example, consider a person who was faithful to the Lord, but began concentrating on his business so much that he skips Sunday services a couple of times. Later he ends up not keeping the Lord's Day at all.

Because of this, God cannot protect him, and he faces a great problem in his business. He may also face an unexpected accident or disease, and it costs him a fortune. This kind of case is like the plague of hail.

Most people consider their fortune as precious as their lives. In 1 Timothy 6:10 it is said that the love of money is the root of all evil. It is because the desire for money results in murders, robberies, abductions, violence, and many other crimes. Sometimes, relationship between brothers is broken, and disputes take place among the neighbors because of money. The main reason for conflicts between countries is also material benefits, since they seek land and resources.

Even some believers cannot overcome the temptation of money, so they do not keep the Lord's Day holy, or they do not give proper tithes. Since they are not leading a proper Christian life, they become more distanced from salvation.

Just as hail destroys most of the food, the plague of hail symbolizes great damage to people's wealth that is considered as precious as their lives. But, as hail falls only in limited areas, they are not going to lose all of their fortune.

Through this fact, we can feel the love of God as well. If we completely lose our whole fortune, everything that we have, then we may give up and even commit suicide. That is why God first touches only a part.

Although it is only a part, the magnitude is strong and significant enough that we may finally come to some kind of realization. Especially, the hail that fell on Egypt was not just small pieces of ice. It was quite large, and the speed was very fast as well.

Even today the news reports that the hail as big as golf balls caused alarm and surprise to many people. The hail that fell on Egypt came by the special work of God, and it also fell with fire. It was a very fearful occurrence.

The plague of hail came upon them because Pharaoh piled evil upon evil. If we have hardened and stubborn hearts, we may also face the same kind of plague.

Plague of Locusts

The trees and vegetables were damaged, and the animals and even people died due to the hail. Pharaoh finally acknowledged his fault.

> Then Pharaoh sent for Moses and Aaron, and said to them, "I have sinned this time; the LORD is the righteous one, and I and my people are the wicked ones" (Exodus 9:27).

Pharaoh repented in a hurried manner and asked Moses to stop the hail.

> Make supplication to the LORD, for there has been enough of God's thunder and hail; and I will let you go,

and you shall stay no longer (Exodus 9:28).

Moses knew that Pharaoh still had not changed his mind, but in order to let him understand about the living God and that the whole world was in His hand, he lifted his hands towards the sky.

As Moses expected, as soon as the rain, thunder, and hail stopped, Pharaoh changed his thoughts. Because he did not turn from the bottom of his heart, he hardened his heart again and did not let the Israelites go.

Pharaoh's servants hardened their hearts as well. Then, Moses and Aaron told them that there would be a plague of locusts as God had said, and warned them that it would be one of the greatest plagues that had never before been in the world.

They shall cover the surface of the land, so that no one will be able to see the land (Exodus 10:5).

Only then the servants of Pharaoh had the fear and said to their king, "Let the men go, that they may serve the LORD their God. Do you not realize that Egypt is destroyed?"

Upon the word of his servants, Pharaoh called Moses and Aaron again. But Moses said they would go with their young and their old; with their sons and their daughters, with their flocks and their herds, for they must hold a feast to the LORD. Pharaoh said that Moses and Aaron were evil and he just drove them out.

Finally, God allowed the eighth plague, the plague of locusts.

> *Then the LORD said to Moses, "Stretch out your hand over the land of Egypt for the locusts, that they may come up on the land of Egypt and eat every plant of the land, even all that the hail has left" (Exodus 10:12).*

When Moses did what God said, God directed an east wind on the land all that day and all that night; and when it was morning, the east wind brought the locusts.

Locusts were so numerous that the land became dark. They ate up all the plants of Egypt that the hail had left, and in Egypt, there was nothing green.

> *I have sinned against the LORD your God and against you. "Now therefore, please forgive my sin only this once, and make supplication to the LORD your God, that He would only remove this death from me" (Exodus 10:16-17).*

When his worry was realized, Pharaoh hurriedly called for Moses and Aaron to make the request to stop the plague.

When Moses went out and prayed to God, there was a strong west wind and put all the locusts in the Red Sea. And there was no locust in all the lands of Egypt. But even this time, Pharaoh hardened his heart and did not send out the Israelites.

The Spiritual Meaning of the Plague of Locusts

A single locust is just a small insect, but when it swarms in a big group, it is devastating. In a moment, Egypt was almost destroyed by the locusts.

> *The locusts came up over all the land of Egypt and settled in all the territory of Egypt; they were very numerous. There had never been so many locusts, nor would there be so many again. For they covered the surface of the whole land, so that the land was darkened; and they ate every plant of the land and all the fruit of the trees that the hail had left. Thus nothing green was left on tree or plant of the field through all the land of Egypt (Exodus 10:14-15).*

Even today, we can find this kind of swarming in Africa or India. The locusts spread up to 40 km in width and 8 km in depth. Hundreds of millions of them come like a cloud and eat up not only the crops, but also all plants and leaves; they leave no green vegetation behind.

After the plague of hail, there were still some things remaining. The wheat and the spelt were not ruined, for they ripen late. Also, some servants of Pharaoh who feared the word of God made their servants and their livestock flee into the houses, and they were not destroyed.

Locusts may not look like very much, but the damage is

much greater than the plague of hail. They ate up even the things that were remaining.

Therefore, the plague of locusts refers to the kind of disasters that do not leave anything behind, taking away all one's wealth and possessions. It destroys not only the family but also workplaces and businesses.

Unlike the plague of hail that gives us partial damage, the plague of locusts destroys everything and takes away all the money. In other words, one will be completely devastated financially.

For example, due to bankruptcy, one loses all his fortune and he has to be separated from his family members. One may also suffer from a long-lasting disease and lose all his fortune. There may be another who comes to have a great amount of debt because his children go wrong.

When they face continuous disasters, some people think that they may be some kind of coincidence, but there is no coincidence in the sight of God. When one faces damage or gets a disease, there must be a reason.

What does it mean if believers face these kinds of disasters? When they hear the word of God and come to know the will of God, they have to keep the word. But if they keep on acting evil just like unbelievers, they cannot avoid these plagues.

If they don't realize when God shows them some signs a couple of times, God will turn His face away from them. Then, a disease may develop into a pestilence, or boils may erupt.

Later, they will face plagues like the plagues of hail or locusts.

But the wise ones will understand that it is the love of God that allows them to realize their faults when they face little disasters. They will quickly repent and avoid greater plagues.

There is a real-life story. One person suffered from a great difficulty for he had once caused God to be enraged. One day, due to fire, he came to have a great amount of debt. His wife could not endure the pressure from the creditors and attempted to commit suicide. In time, however, they came to know God and began to attend the church.

After they had counseling with me, they obeyed the word of God with prayers. They pleased God by doing voluntary works in the church. Then, their problems were solved one by one, and they didn't have to suffer from the creditors anymore. Furthermore, they paid off all their debts. They were even able to build a commercial building and buy a house.

After all their difficulties were resolved and they received blessings, however, they changed their hearts. They forsook the grace of God and became just like unbelievers again.

One day, a part of the building that the husband owned collapsed due to flooding. There was also a fire again, and he lost everything financially. Having again incurred a great amount of debt, they had to go back to their hometown in countryside. But he also had diabetes and the complications along with it.

Like in this case, if we are left with nothing after trying all the methods with our knowledge and wisdom, we have to go before God with humble heart. As we reflect ourselves on the word of God, repent of our sins, and turn away, the previous things will be recovered.

If we have the faith to come before God and commit every matter into God's hands, the God of love who does not break the bruised reed will forgive us and recover us. If we turn around and live in the light, God will guide us to prosperity once again and give us greater blessings.

Chapter 6

Plagues of Darkness
and Death of the Firstborn

Exodus 10:22-12:36

So Moses stretched out his hand toward the sky, and there was thick darkness in all the land of Egypt for three days. They did not see one another, nor did anyone rise from his place for three days, but all the sons of Israel had light in their dwellings (10:22-23)
Now it came about at midnight that the LORD struck all the firstborn in the land of Egypt, from the firstborn of Pharaoh who sat on his throne to the firstborn of the captive who was in the dungeon, and all the firstborn of cattle. Pharaoh arose in the night, he and all his servants and all the Egyptians, and there was a great cry in Egypt, for there was no home where there was not someone dead (12:29-30).

In the Bible we can find that when they face difficulties many people repented before God and received His help.

God sent his prophet to King Hezekiah of the Kingdom of Judah and said, "You shall die and not live." But the king prayed earnestly with his tears, and his life was extended.

Nineveh was the capital city of Assyria, which was a hostile country toward Israel. When the people there heard the word of God through His prophet, they thoroughly repented of their sins and were not destroyed.

Likewise, God gives His mercy to those who turn back. He searches those who seek His grace and gives more grace to them.

Pharaoh suffered from various plagues due to his evil, but he did not turn around until the end. The more he hardened his heart, the greater the plagues became.

Plague of Darkness

Some people say that they would never live if they lose. They believe in their own strength. Pharaoh was this kind of a person. He considered himself to be a god, and that's why he did not want to acknowledge God.

Even after seeing the whole land of Egypt was destroyed, he did not send out the Israelites. He was acting as if he were competing with God. Then, God allowed the plague of darkness.

> *So Moses stretched out his hand toward the sky, and there was thick darkness in all the land of Egypt for three days. They did not see one another, nor did anyone rise from his place for three days, but all the sons of Israel had light in their dwellings (Exodus 10:22-23).*

The darkness was so thick that they could not see one another. Nobody got up and moved around from where he was for three days. How can we express the full extent of the fear and discomfort they had to face for three days?

The thick darkness covered all the lands of Egypt and the people had to walk in blindness, but in the land of Goshen the sons of Israel had light in their dwellings.

Pharaoh called for Moses and said he would release the Israelites. But, he told Moses to leave the flocks and herds, and take only the sons and daughters. Actually it was his intention to retain the Israelites.

But Moses said that they had to have the animals to sacrifice to God, and they could not leave any because they would not know which one they would sacrifice to God.

Again Pharaoh became angry and even threatened Moses saying, "Do not see my face again, for in the day you see my face you shall die!"

Moses boldly replied, "You are right; I shall never see your face again!" and he went out.

Spiritual Meaning of the Plague of Darkness

The spiritual meaning of the plague of darkness is spiritual darkness, and it refers to the plague just before death.

It is a case in which a disease has become so serious that the person cannot recover. It is the kind of plague that comes upon those who do not repent even after losing all their fortunes that are like their lives.

Standing at the threshold of death is like standing on the edge of a cliff in total darkness and not having any way out of the predicament. Spiritually, because one has forsaken God and completely abandoned his faith, God's grace is taken away from him, and his spiritual life comes to an end. But, God still has His compassion on him and has not taken his life.

In a case of an unbeliever, a person may face this kind of situation because he has not accepted God yet, even after suffering from many kinds of disasters. In case of believers, it is because they did not keep the word of God, but piled up evil upon evil.

We often find that some people have spent fortunes on the healing of their diseases but are still just awaiting death. These are the ones who are struck with the plague of darkness.

They also suffer from neurotic problems like depression, insomnia, and nervous breakdowns. They feel helpless difficulties in continuing their daily existences.

If they realize, repent of, and turn back from their evils, God has mercy on them and takes away the disastrous anguish from them.

But in case of the Pharaoh, he hardened his heart even more to stand against God to the end. It's the same today. Some stubborn people do not come before God in no matter what kind of difficulties they are. When they or their family members have been stricken with serious disease, lost all their fortune, and now their lives are in peril, they do not want to repent before God.

If we continue to stand against God even in the midst of many disasters, finally, the plague of death will be inflicted.

Plague of Death of the Firstborn

God let Moses know what would happen next in the Exodus.

> *One more plague I will bring on Pharaoh and on Egypt; after that he will let you go from here. When he lets you go, he will surely drive you out from here completely. Speak now in the hearing of the people that each man ask from his neighbor and each woman from her neighbor for articles of silver and articles of gold (Exodus 11:1-2).*

Moses was in a situation where he could even be killed if he was to go before Pharaoh again, but he stood before Pharaoh to deliver the will of God.

And all the firstborn in the land of Egypt shall die, from the firstborn of the Pharaoh who sits on his throne, even to the firstborn of the slave girl who is behind the millstones; all the firstborn of the cattle as well. Moreover, there shall be a great cry in all the land of Egypt, such as there has not been before and such as shall never be again (Exodus 11:5-6).

Then as spoken, in the night, all the firstborn of not only Pharaoh and his servants but everybody in Egypt; and all the livestock died.

There was a great cry in Egypt, for there was no home of which the firstborn was not dead. Because Pharaoh hardened his heart to the end and not turned, the plague of death even came upon them.

Spiritual Meaning of the Plague of Death of the Firstborn

Plague of death of the firstborn refers to a situation where a person himself, or his most loved one, possibly his child, or one among his family members, dies, or gets into a way of complete destruction and not being able to receive salvation.

We can find this kind of case in the Bible, too. The first king of Israel, Saul disobeyed the word of God telling him to destroy everything in Amalek. Also, he showed his arrogance by offering sacrifice to God himself, which only priests could do. Finally, he was forsaken by God.

In this kind of situation, rather than realizing his sins and repenting, he tried to kill his faithful servant David. When people followed David, deeper and deeper he fell into the evil thought that David would rebel against him.

So, even when David was playing the harps for him, Saul threw a spear to kill David. He also sent David to a battle that was impossible for him to win. He even sent his soldiers to David's house to kill him.

Furthermore, just because they helped David, he killed the priests of God. He accumulated many evil acts. Finally, he lost a battle and died a miserable death. By his own hand he killed himself.

How about the priest Eli and his sons? Eli was a priest in Israel at the time of the judges, and was to set a good example. But his sons Hophni and Phinehas were worthless men who did not know God (1 Samuel 2:12).

Since their father was a priest, they also had to do the work of serving God, but they despised the offering of God. They touched the meat of the offering-sacrifice before it was given to

God, and even lay with the women who served at the doorway of the tent of meeting.

If the children go the wrong way, the parents have to admonish them, and if they don't listen, the parents have to implement stricter measures to stop their children. It is the duty and true love of the parents. But the priest Eli only said, "Why do you do such things? No."

His sons did not turn back from their sins, and curses fell on his family. His two sons were killed in a battle.

Hearing this news, Eli fell from the chair and broke his neck and died. Also, his daughter-in-law had a shock in her early delivery and finally died.

Just by seeing these cases, we can understand that curses or tragic deaths do not just come without cause.

When one lives a life of disobedience against God's word, he or some of his family members face death. Some people come back before God only after seeing such deaths.

If they do not turn away even after facing the plague of death of the firstborn, they cannot be saved forever, and it is the greatest plague. Therefore, before any plagues come, and if the plagues have come already, you have to repent of your sins before it is too late.

In the case of Pharaoh, only after he suffered from all ten plagues did he acknowledge God with fear and let the people of Israel go.

> Then [Pharaoh] called for Moses and Aaron at night and said, "Rise up, get out from among my people, both you and the sons of Israel; and go, worship the LORD, as you have said. Take both your flocks and your herds, as you have said, and go, and bless me also" (Exodus 12:31-32).

Through the Ten Plagues, Pharaoh clearly showed his hardened heart and was forced to release the Israelites. But he soon regretted it. He changed his mind again. He took all his army and the chariots of Egypt and chased the Israelites.

> So he made his chariot ready and took his people with him; and he took six hundred select chariots, and all the other chariots of Egypt with officers over all of them. The LORD hardened the heart of Pharaoh, king of Egypt, and he chased after the sons of Israel as the sons of Israel were going out boldly (Exodus 14:6-8).

It was good enough to submit to God after he experienced the deaths of firstborns, but he soon regretted sending out the Israelites. He took his army to pursue them. By seeing this, we can realize how hardened and cunning man's heart can be. Finally, God did not forgive him and had no other choice but to let them die in the waters of the Red Sea.

> Then the LORD said to Moses, "Stretch out your hand

over the sea so that the waters may come back over the Egyptians, over their chariots and their horsemen." So Moses stretched out his hand over the sea, and the sea returned to its normal state at daybreak, while the Egyptians were fleeing right into it; then the LORD overthrew the Egyptians in the midst of the sea. The waters returned and covered the chariots and the horsemen, even Pharaoh's entire army that had gone into the sea after them; not even one of them remained (Exodus 14:26-28).

Even today, evil people will beg for a chance when they are in a difficult situation. But when they are actually given a chance, they return to their evil again. When evil continues this way, they will finally face death.

Life of Disobedience and Life of Obedience

There is one important thing that we have to clearly understand; it is that when we have done wrong and realize it, we must not add to the evil with any further evil, but walk in the way of righteousness.

1 Peter 5:8-9 says, *"Be of sober spirit, be on the alert. Your adversary, the devil, prowls around like a roaring lion, seeking someone to devour. But resist him, firm in your faith, knowing that the same experiences of suffering are being accomplished*

by your brethren who are in the world."

1 John 5:18 also says, *"We know that no one who is born of God sins; but He who was born of God keeps him, and the evil one does not touch him."*

Therefore, if we do not commit sins but live in the word of God perfectly, God will protect us with His blazing eyes, so that we will not have to worry about anything.

Around us, we can see people face many kinds of disasters, but they do not even understand why they are facing many difficulties. Also, we can see some believers suffering from many hardships.

Some face plagues of blood or gnats, some others plagues of hail or locusts. Still others face the plague of death of firstborn, and furthermore, they face the plague of water-burial.

Therefore, we should not live a life of disobedience like Pharaoh but a life of obedience, so that we will not face any of these plagues.

Even if we are in a situation where we cannot avoid facing the plague of death of the firstborn or the plague of darkness, we can be forgiven if we repent and turn away from the sin right now. Just as with the Egyptian army that was buried in the Red Sea, if we delay any longer and do not turn back, there will be a time that comes when it will be too late.

On Life of Obedience

Now it shall be, if you diligently obey the LORD your God,
being careful to do all His commandments
which I command you today,
the LORD your God will set you high
above all the nations of the earth.
All these blessings will come upon you
and overtake you if you obey
the LORD your God: Blessed shall you be in the city,
and blessed shall you be in the country.
Blessed shall be the offspring of your body
and the produce of your ground
and the offspring of your beasts,
the increase of your herd and the young of your flock.
Blessed shall be your basket and your kneading bowl.
Blessed shall you be when you come in,
and blessed shall you be when you go out.
(Deuteronomy 28:1-6)

Chapter 7

Passover and Way of Salvation

Exodus 12:1-28

Now the LORD said to Moses and Aaron in the land of Egypt, "This month shall be the beginning of months for you; it is to be the first month of the year to you. Speak to all the congregation of Israel, saying, 'On the tenth of this month they are each one to take a lamb for themselves, according to their fathers' households, a lamb for each household'" (1-3).

"You shall keep it until the fourteenth day of the same month, then the whole assembly of the congregation of Israel is to kill it at twilight. Moreover, they shall take some of the blood and put it on the two doorposts and on the lintel of the houses in which they eat it. They shall eat the flesh that same night, roasted with fire, and they shall eat it with unleavened bread and bitter herbs. Do not eat any of it raw or boiled at all with water, but rather roasted with fire, both its head and its legs along with its entrails. And you shall not leave any of it over until morning, but whatever is left of it until morning, you shall burn with fire. Now you shall eat it in this manner: with your loins girded, your sandals on your feet, and your staff in your hand; and you shall eat it in haste it is the LORD's Passover" (6-11).

Up to this point, we can see that Pharaoh and his servants continued to live lives in disobedience to the word of God.

As a result, there were minor plagues on all lands of Egypt. As they continued to disobey, many diseases were inflicted, their fortune disappeared, and finally they lost their lives.

In contrast, even though they lived in the same country of Egypt, the chosen people of Israel did not suffer any of the plagues.

When God struck the lives in Egypt with the last plague, the Israelites did not have any loss of life. It was because God had let the people of Israel know the way to salvation.

This does not only apply to the people of Israel many thousands of years ago, but in the same way it is still just as applicable to us today.

The Way to Avoid the Plague of Death of the Firstborn

Before there was the plague of death of the firstborn in Egypt, God told Israelites the way to avoid the plague.

> *Speak to all the congregation of Israel, saying, "On the tenth of this month they are each one to take a lamb for themselves, according to their fathers' households, a lamb for each household" (Exodus 12:3).*

Beginning with the plague of blood through the plague

of darkness, even though the people of Israel had not done anything by themselves, God just protected them with His power. But just before the last plague, God wanted some act of obedience from the people of Israel.

It was to take a lamb and put some blood on two doorposts and on the lintel of the houses, and eat the lamb roasted over fire in the house. This was the sign to distinguish the people of God when God would kill all the firstborn of the men and animals of Egypt.

Because the last plague passed over the houses that had the blood of the lamb, the Jews still celebrate this day as the Passover, on which they were saved.

Today, Passover is the biggest feast of the Jews. They eat lamb, unleavened bread and bitter herbs to celebrate this day. More details will be explained in chapter 8.

Take a Lamb

God told them to take a lamb because the lamb spiritually stands for Jesus Christ.

Generally speaking, those who believe in God are called His 'sheep.' Many people think that the 'lamb' is a 'new-believer,' but in the Bible, we can find that the 'lamb' refers to Jesus Christ.

In John 1:29, John the Baptist said, pointing to Jesus, *"Behold, the Lamb of God who takes away the sin of the world!"* 1 Peter 1:18-19 says, *"You were not redeemed with perishable things like silver or gold from your futile way of life inherited from your forefathers, but with precious blood, as of a lamb unblemished and spotless, the blood of Christ."*

Jesus' character and deeds remind us of a gentle lamb. Matthew 12:19-20 also says, *"He will not quarrel, nor cry out; nor will anyone hear His voice in the streets. A battered reed He will not break off, and a smoldering wick He will not put out, until He leads justice to victory."*

Just as a sheep hears only the voice of its shepherd and follows him, Jesus only obeyed with 'Yes' and 'Amen' before God (Revelation 3:14). Until He died on the cross, He wanted to fulfill the will of God (Luke 22:42).

A lamb gives us soft fur, highly nutritious milk and meat. Likewise, Jesus also was offered as an atoning sacrifice to reconcile us with God as He shed all His water and blood on the cross.

Thus, many parts of the Bible liken Jesus with a lamb. When God instructed the Israelites in the customs of the Passover, He also told them how to partake of the lamb in detail.

> *Now if the household is too small for a lamb, then he and his neighbor nearest to his house are to take one according to the number of persons in them; according to what each man should eat, you are to divide the lamb. 'Your lamb shall be an unblemished male a year old; you may take it from the sheep or from the goats (Exodus 12:4-5).*

If they were too poor, or there were not enough members in the family to eat a whole lamb, they could take one lamb from either a sheep or goat, and they could share the one lamb with a neighboring family. We can feel the delicate love of God who is abundant in compassion.

The reason why God told them to take an unblemished male a year old is because its meat is the most delicious at this time for it has not yet mated. Also, as it is in the case for men, it is the time of the youth, being most beautiful and clean.

Because God is holy without any blemish or spot, He told them to take the lamb of the most beautiful time, a one-year old lamb.

Apply Blood and Do Not Go Outside until Morning

God said that they had to take a lamb according to the numbers in their households. In Exodus 12:6 we find that they were not to kill the lamb immediately, but after keeping it for four days, at twilight it was to be done. God gave them a period of time to prepare for it with all the sincerity of their hearts.

Why did God say they had to kill it at twilight?

Human cultivation, which began with the disobedience of Adam, can be generally categorized into three parts. From

Adam to Abraham is about 2,000 years, and this period of time is the beginning stage of human cultivation. In comparison with one day, it is morning.

After that, God appointed Abraham as the father of faith, and from the time of Abraham until Jesus came to this earth, it is also about 2,000 years. This is like the daytime.

From the time Jesus came to this earth until today, it is also about 2,000 years. This is the end time of human cultivation and the twilight of the day (1 John 2:18; Jude 1:18; Hebrews 1:2; 1 Peter 1:5; 20).

The time when Jesus came to this earth and redeemed us from our sins through his death for us upon the cross belongs to the last era of human cultivation, and that is why God told them to kill the lamb at the twilight and not during the day.

Then, the people were supposed to apply the blood of the lamb on two doorposts and the lintel (Exodus 12:7). The blood of the lamb spiritually refers to the blood of Jesus Christ. God told them to apply the blood on two doorposts and the lintel because we are saved by the blood of Jesus. By shedding blood and dying on the cross, Jesus redeemed us from our sins and saved our lives; this is the spiritual meaning that is implied.

Because it is the holy blood that redeems us from sins, they were not supposed to apply the blood on the threshold on which people step, but only on the doorposts and lintel.

Jesus said, *"I am the door; if anyone enters through Me, he will be saved, and will go in and out and find pasture"* (John

10:9). As said, on the night of the plague of firstborn's death, all the households that did not have the blood, had deaths in them, but those households that applied blood were saved from death.

But even if they applied the blood of the lamb, if they went outside the door, they could not be saved (Exodus 12:22). If they went outside of the door, it means they had nothing to do with the covenant of God, and they had to face the plague of death of the firstborn.

Spiritually, outside the doors symbolizes darkness that has nothing to do with God. It is the world of untruths. In the same way, today, even if we have accepted the Lord, we cannot be saved if we leave Him.

Roast the Lamb and Eat it as a Whole

There were deaths in the households of Egyptians, and there was a great cry. Starting from the Pharaoh, who did not fear God at all even after so many powerful works of God were shown to all Egyptians, a great cry broke out in the silence of the deep night.

But until morning, the Israelites did not go outside the doors at all. They just ate the lamb according to the word of God. What is the reason that they had to eat the meat of the lamb at late night? This contains a deep spiritual meaning.

Before Adam ate from the tree of the knowledge of good

and evil, he lived under the control of God who is light, but since he disobeyed and ate from the tree, he became a servant of sin. Due to this, all his descendants, all mankind, came under the control of the enemy devil and Satan, the ruler of darkness. Therefore, this world is of the darkness or night.

Just as the Israelites had to eat the lamb at late night, we who are spiritually living in the world of darkness have to eat the flesh of the Son of Man, which is the word of God who is light, and drink His blood, so that we can receive salvation. God told them in detail how to eat the lamb. They had to eat it with unleavened bread and bitter herbs (Exodus 12:8).

Yeast is a kind of fungus which is used to make bread rise, and it ferments the food to make it more delicious and soft. Bread without yeast is less delicious than bread made with it.

Since it was such a desperate situation of whether to live or not to live, God let them eat the lamb with less delicious unleavened bread and bitter herbs to let them remember the day.

Also, yeast refers to sins and evil in a spiritual sense. Therefore, 'to eat the unleavened bread that is without the yeast' symbolizes that we have to remove sins and evil to receive the salvation of life.

And God told them to roast the lamb over the fire, not to eat it raw or boiled in water, and they were to eat it all, the head, the legs, and the entrails (Exodus 12:9).

Here, 'to eat it raw' means interpreting the precious word of God literally.

For example, Matthew 6:6 says, *"But you, when you pray, go into your inner room, close your door and pray to your Father who is in secret, and your Father who sees what is done in secret will reward you."* If we interpret it literally, we have to go into inner room, close the door, and pray. But nowhere in the Bible can we find any man of God praying in inner rooms with the door closed.

Spiritually, 'to go into inner room and pray' means that we must not have any idle thoughts, but pray with all our hearts.

In our diet, if we eat raw meat, we may have some infections from parasites or we may get a stomachache. If we interpret the word of God literally, we come to have misunderstandings and it leads to problems. Then, we cannot have spiritual faith, so that it even leads us farther from salvation.

'To boil it in water' means 'to add philosophy, science, medical science, or human thoughts to the word of God.' If we boil the meat in water, the juice of meat will come out and there is a great loss of the nutrients. In the same way, if we add the knowledge of this world to the word of truth, we may have some faith as knowledge, but we cannot have spiritual faith. Therefore, it does not lead us to salvation.

Now, what does it mean by roasting the lamb over the fire? Here, 'fire' stands for the 'fire of the Holy Spirit.' Namely, the word of God was written in the inspiration of the Holy Spirit, and therefore, when we hear and read it, we have to do it within the fullness and inspiration of the Holy Spirit. Otherwise, it will only become a piece of knowledge, and we cannot get it as spiritual bread.

In order to eat the word of God roasted over fire, we must have fervent prayers. Prayer is like oil, and it is the source to give us the fullness of the Holy Spirit. When we take the word of God with the inspiration of the Holy Spirit, the word will taste sweeter than honey. It means that we are listening to the word with thirsting heart like a deer pants for a stream of water. Thus, we feel that the time to listen to the word of God is so precious, and we will never feel it boring.

When we listen to the word of God, if we utilize man's thoughts, or our own experience and knowledge, we may not understand many things.

For example, God tells us, if anyone strikes one of our cheeks, to turn to him the other also, and if anyone asks for a tunic, to give him the cloak as well, and if anyone forces us to go with him one mile, to go with him two miles. Also, many people think it is right to take revenge, but God tells us to love even our enemies, humble ourselves, and serve others (Matthew 5:39-44).

That is why we have to break all our thoughts and take the word of God only within the inspiration of the Holy Spirit. Only then will the word of God become our life and strength, so that we will be able to cast off untruths and we will be guided to the way of eternal life.

Generally, it tastes better when we roast meat on fire, and it is a way to prevent infections. In the same way, the enemy devil and Satan cannot work on those who take the word of God spiritually with the feeling that it is sweeter than honey.

Furthermore, God told them to eat the head, its legs, and entrails. This means that we have to take all the sixty-six books of the Bible, without leaving out any of them.

The Bible contains the origin of creation and the providence of human cultivation. Moreover, it contains the ways to become God's true children. It contains the providence of salvation that had been hidden since before time began. The Bible contains the will of God.

Therefore, 'to eat the head, the legs, and entrails' means that we have to take the Bible as a whole beginning with the Book of Genesis to the Book of Revelation.

Do Not Leave Any of It Until Morning, Eat in Haste

The people of Israel ate the lamb roasted over the fire at their homes, and they didn't leave any of it until morning, for Exodus 12:10 says, *"And you shall not leave any of it over until morning, but whatever is left of it until morning, you shall burn with fire."*

'Morning' is when the darkness goes away and the light comes. Spiritually, it refers to the time of the second coming of the Lord. After He comes back, we cannot prepare our oil (Matthew 25:1-13), and so, we have to take the word of God diligently and practice it before the Lord Jesus comes back.

Also, men can live only for seventy or eighty years, and we don't know when our lives will end. Therefore, we have to diligently take the word of God all the time.

The people of Israel had to depart from Egypt after the plague of death of the firstborn took place, and that is why God told them to eat in haste.

> *Now you shall eat it in this manner: with your loins girded, your sandals on your feet, and your staff in your hand; and you shall eat it in haste it is the LORD's Passover (Exodus 12:11).*

This means that they had to get ready to leave with all their clothes and shoes on. To have loins girded and to put on the sandals means that they had to be fully ready.

In order to receive salvation through Jesus Christ in this world, which is like Egypt that was plagued by pains, and to enter into heavenly kingdom, which is like the Promised Land of Canaan, we also have to be always awake and ready.

Also God told them to have their staff in their hand, and the 'staff' spiritually symbolizes 'faith.' When we walk or climb a mountain, if we have a staff, it will be much safer and easier, and we will not fall down.

The reason the staff was given to Moses was because Moses

had not received the Holy Spirit in heart. God gave Moses the staff that spiritually stood for faith. That way the people of Israel could experience the power of God through a staff that was physically seen by eyes, and the work of the Exodus from Egypt could be accomplished.

Even today, to enter into eternal heavenly kingdom, we have to possess spiritual faith. We can reach salvation only when we believe in the Lord Jesus Christ who died on the cross without any sin and resurrected. We can reach complete salvation only when we practice the word of God by eating the flesh of the Lord and drinking His blood.

Moreover, now is the time that is ever so near for the Lord to come back. Thus, we have to obey the word of God and pray fervently so that we can always win the victory in the battles against the forces of darkness.

> *Therefore, take up the full armor of God, so that you will be able to resist in the evil day, and having done everything, to stand firm. Stand firm therefore, having girded your loins with truth, and having put on the breastplate of righteousness, and having shod your feet with the preparation of the gospel of peace; in addition to all, taking up the shield of faith with which you will be able to extinguish all the flaming arrows of the evil one. And take the helmet of salvation, and the sword of the Spirit, which is the word of God (Ephesians 6:13-17).*

Chapter 8

Circumcision and Holy Communion

Exodus 12:43-51

The LORD said to Moses and Aaron, "This is the ordinance of the Passover" (43).

But no uncircumcised person may eat of it (48).

"The same law shall apply to the native as to the stranger who sojourns among you"(49).

And on that same day the LORD brought the sons of Israel out of the land of Egypt by their hosts (51).

The celebration the Feast of the Passover has been kept for the longest continuous period of time in the world, for more than 3,500 years. It was the foundation of the establishment of the country Israel.

Passover is פסח (Pesach) in Hebrew, and it means, as name says, passing over or forgiving something. It means that the shadow of darkness passed over the houses of Israel whose doorposts and lintel were covered with the blood of the lamb when the plague of death of the firstborn came upon Egypt.

In Israel, even today, they clean the houses and remove all the leavened bread from the house at Passover. Even little children search underneath the beds or behind the furniture with flashlights for any snacks or bread that has yeast in it, and remove it. Also, each household eats according to the regulations of the Passover. The head of the family brings the Feast of the Passover to remembrance, and they celebrate the Exodus.

"Why do we eat Matzo (unleavened bread) tonight?"

"Why do we eat Maror (bitter herbs) tonight?"

"Why do we eat parsley after dipping it into salt-water two times? Why do we eat bitter herbs with Harosheth (A reddish color jam, symbolizing the baking the bricks in Egypt)?"

"Why do we lie back and eat the Passover food?"

The leader of the ceremony explains that they had to eat

unleavened bread for they had to leave Egypt in haste. Also, he explains about eating the bitter herbs to remember the pain of slavery in Egypt, and eating the parsley dipped in salt-water to remember the tears they had shed in Egypt.

But now, since their fathers were set free from the slavery, they eat the food lying back to express the freedom and joy of being able to recline while eating. And when the leader talks about the stories of the ten plagues in Egypt, each of the family members holds a little bit of wine in their mouths whenever the name of the plague is mentioned, and then spits it out to a separate bowl.

The Passover took place 3,500 years ago, but through the food of the Passover, even the children now have a chance to experience the Exodus. The Jews are still observing this feast that God had established thousands of years ago.

The power of Diaspora, namely the power for the Jews who were scattered around the world to come back together and reestablish their country, lies here.

Qualifications for the Participants in the Passover

On the night the plague of death of the firstborn came upon Egypt, Israelites were saved from death by obeying the word of God. But to participate in Passover, they had to meet a condition.

CIRCUMCISION AND HOLY COMMUNION · 111

The LORD said to Moses and Aaron, "This is the ordinance of the Passover: no foreigner is to eat of it; but every man's slave purchased with money, after you have circumcised him, then he may eat of it. A sojourner or a hired servant shall not eat of it. It is to be eaten in a single house; you are not to bring forth any of the flesh outside of the house, nor are you to break any bone of it. All the congregation of Israel are to celebrate this. But if a stranger sojourns with you, and celebrates the Passover to the LORD, let all his males be circumcised, and then let him come near to celebrate it; and he shall be like a native of the land. But no uncircumcised person may eat of it. The same law shall apply to the native as to the stranger who sojourns among you" (Exodus 12:43-49).

Only those who were circumcised could eat the Passover food, for circumcision is a crucial thing for life, and spiritually related to the matter of salvation.

Circumcision is the removal of some or the entire foreskin (prepuce) from the penis and is done on the 8th day since birth of all male babies of Israel.

Genesis 17:9-10 says, *"And God said to Abraham: 'As for you, you shall keep My covenant, you and your descendants after you throughout their generations. This is My covenant which you shall keep, between Me and you and your descendants after you: Every male child among you shall be circumcised.'"*

When God gave His covenant of blessings to Abraham, the father of faith, He asked him to perform the circumcision as the sigh of the covenant. Those who were not circumcised could not receive the blessings.

> *And you shall be circumcised in the flesh of your foreskin, and it shall be the sign of the covenant between Me and you. And every male among you who is eight days old shall be circumcised throughout your generations, a servant who is born in the house or who is bought with money from any foreigner, who is not of your descendants. A servant who is born in your house or who is bought with your money shall surely be circumcised; thus shall My covenant be in your flesh for an everlasting covenant. But an uncircumcised male who is not circumcised in the flesh of his foreskin, that person shall be cut off from his people; he has broken My covenant (Genesis 17:11-14).*

Then, why did God command them to get circumcised on the eighth day?

When a baby is newly born after being in the mother's womb for nine months, it is not easy for him to apply himself to everything new around him because the environment is very different. The cells are still weak, but after seven days, they become familiarized with the new environment, but still they are not very active yet.

If the foreskin is cut off at this time, the pain is the minimum, and the cut will be closed very quickly. But after one grows up, the skin is hard and it will be very painful.

God made the Israelites conduct the circumcision on the 8th day after birth, so that it would be helpful for the sanitation and growth, making it the sign of His covenant at the same time.

Circumcision, Directly Related with Life

Exodus 4:24-26 says, *"And it came to pass on the way, at the encampment, that the LORD met [Moses] and sought to kill him. Then Zipporah took a sharp stone and cut off the foreskin of her son and cast it at Moses' feet, and said, 'Surely you are a husband of blood to me!' So He let him go. Then she said, 'You are a husband of blood!'-- because of the circumcision."*

Why did God seek to kill Moses?

We can understand it if we understand the birth and growth of Moses. At that time, to destroy the Israelites completely, an order was given to kill all the new-born Hebrew boys.

During this time, Moses' mother hid him. She finally put him in a wicker basket and put it by the bank of the Nile. By the providence of God, he was seen by an Egyptian princess and he also became a prince as an adopted son of the princess. That is why he was not in a situation to get circumcised.

Although he was called as the leader of the Exodus, he was not circumcised yet. That is why the angel of God sought to kill him. Likewise, circumcision is directly related with life; if one is not circumcised, he has nothing to do with God.

Hebrews 10:1 says, *"For the law, having a shadow of the good things to come, and not the very image of the things,"* and the law here refers to the Old Testament, and the 'things to come' is the New Testament, namely the Good News coming through Jesus Christ.

Shadow and the original image are one, and they cannot exist separately. Therefore, the commandment of God about circumcision in the Old Testament times, which governed that they would be cut off from among the people of God without circumcision, still applies to us in the same way today.

But today, unlike in the Old Testament, we do not have to undergo physical circumcision but spiritual circumcision, which is the circumcision of heart.

Physical Circumcision and Circumcision of the Heart

Romans 2:28-29 says, *"For he is not a Jew who is one outwardly, nor is circumcision that which is outward in the flesh; but he is a Jew who is one inwardly; and circumcision is that of the heart, in the Spirit, not in the letter; whose praise is not from men but from God."* Physical circumcision is just a shadow, and the original image in the New Testament is the circumcision of heart, and this is what gives salvation to us.

In Old Testament times, they didn't receive the Holy Spirit, and they could not cast off untruths from their hearts. Thus, they showed that they belonged to God by being physically circumcised. But in New Testament times, when we accept Jesus Christ, the Holy Spirit comes into our heart, and the Holy Spirit helps us to live by the truth so that we can cast off untruths of the heart.

To circumcise our heart this way is to follow the commandment in the Old Testament to be circumcised in body. It is also a way to keep the Passover.

> *Circumcise yourselves to the LORD, And take away the foreskins of your hearts (Jeremiah 4:4).*

What does it mean by taking away the foreskins of the heart? It is to keep all the words of God telling us to do, not to do, to keep, or to cast away certain things.

We just don't do the things that God tells us not to do such as "Do not hate, do not judge or condemn, do not steal, and do not commit adultery." Also, we just cast away and keep when He tells us to cast away or keep something, such as "Cast off all forms of evil, keep the Sabbath, keep the commandments of God."

Also, we just do what He tells us to do such as "Preach the gospel, pray, forgive, love, etc." By doing so, we drive away all untruths, evil, unrighteousness, lawlessness, and darkness from our heart to make it clean, and then we fill it with the truth.

Circumcision of Heart and Complete Salvation

At the time of Moses, the Passover was established for the Israelites to avoid the deaths of the firstborn before the Exodus. Thus, it does not mean that one is forever saved just by participating in the Passover.

If they were saved eternally by the Passover, then all the Israelites who came out of Egypt would have entered into the Land flowing with milk and honey, the Land of Canaan.

But the reality was that the adults, except for Joshua and Caleb, who were above twenty at the time of Exodus, did not show faith and deeds of obedience. They were the generation that had to stay in the wilderness for forty years and die there, without seeing the blessed land Canaan.

It's the same today. Even if we have accepted Jesus Christ, and become children of God, it is not complete and guaranteed forever. It just means that we have entered within the boundary of salvation.

Therefore, just as the forty years of trial was necessary for the Israelites to enter into the Canaan Land, to receive permanent salvation we need to go through a process to be circumcised with the word of God.

Once we accept Jesus Christ as our personal Savior, we receive the Holy Spirit. However, 'to receive the Holy Spirit' does not mean that our heart will be completely clean. We have to keep on circumcising our hearts until we reach complete salvation. Only when we keep our hearts, which is the source of life, through circumcision in heart, can we reach complete salvation.

Importance of Circumcision of Heart

Only when we cleanse away our sins and evils with the word of God and cut it off with the sword of the Holy Spirit, can we become holy children of God and lead the life that is free of disasters.

Another reason why we have to circumcise our hearts is to win the victory in spiritual battles. Though invisible, there are constant and fierce battles between the spirits of goodness belonging to God and evil spirits.

Ephesians 6:12 says, *"For we do not wrestle against flesh and blood, but against principalities, against powers, against the rulers of the darkness of this age, against spiritual hosts of wickedness in the heavenly places."*

To win the victory in this spiritual battle, we absolutely need clean hearts. It's because in spiritual world, the power is in sinlessness. That is why God wants the circumcision of our hearts and He told us many times of the importance of circumcision.

> *Beloved, if our heart does not condemn us, we have confidence toward God. And whatever we ask we receive from Him, because we keep His commandments and do those things that are pleasing in His sight (1 John 3:21-22).*

In order for us to receive the answers to the problems of life such as diseases and poverty, we have to circumcise our hearts. Only when we have clean hearts, will we have confidence before God and receive anything we ask for.

Passover and Holy Communion

Likewise, only when we undergo circumcision can we participate in the Passover. This is related to Holy Communion today. The Passover is a feast to eat the meat of the lamb, and the Holy Communion is to eat the bread and drink wine, which symbolizes the flesh and blood of Jesus.

> *Then Jesus said to them, "Most assuredly, I say to you,*

unless you eat the flesh of the Son of Man and drink His blood, you have no life in you. Whoever eats My flesh and drinks My blood has eternal life, and I will raise him up at the last day" (John 6:53-54).

Here, the 'Son of Man' refers to Jesus, and the flesh of the Son of Man refers to the 66 books of the Bible. To eat the flesh of the Son of Man means to take in the word of the truth of God written in the Bible.

Also, just as we need liquid to help with the digestion of food, when we eat the flesh of the Son of Man, we also have to drink at the same time so it can be digested well.

'To drink the blood of the Son of Man' means to truly believe and to practice the word of God. After hearing and coming to know the word, if we don't practice it, then the word of God is of no use to us.

When we understand the word of God in the sixty-six books of the Bible and practice it, then the truth will come into our heart and be absorbed as nutrients are absorbed by the body. Then, the sins and evil will become as waste to be discarded, so that we will become more and more of men of truth to gain eternal life.

For example, if we take in the nutrient of truth called 'love' and practice it, this word will be absorbed in us as nutrient. The things that are in opposition such as hatred, envy, and jealousy will become as waste to cast off. Then we will come to have a perfect heart of love.

Also, as we fill our heart with peace and righteousness, the quarrels, arguments, dissensions, resentment, and unrighteousness will go away.

Qualifications to Participate in Holy Communion

At the time of Exodus, those who were circumcised were eligible to participate in the Passover, so they could avoid the deaths of the firstborn. In the same way, today, when we accept Jesus Christ as our Savior and receive the Holy Spirit, we are sealed as God's children, and we have the right to participate in Holy Communion.

But the Passover was just for the salvation from the deaths of the firstborn. They still had to march in the wilderness for complete salvation. In the same way, even though we have received the Holy Spirit and can participate in the Holy Communion, we still need to undergo the process to receive eternal salvation for eternity. Since we have come into the gate of salvation by accepting Jesus Christ, we have to obey the word of God in our lives. We have to march towards the gates of the heavenly kingdom and eternal salvation.

If we commit sins, we cannot participate in the Holy Communion to eat the flesh and drink the blood of the Holy Lord. We first have to look back on ourselves, repent of all sins we have committed, and cleanse our hearts to participate in the

Holy Communion.

> *Therefore whoever eats this bread or drinks this cup of the Lord in an unworthy manner will be guilty of the body and blood of the Lord. But let a man examine himself, and so let him eat of the bread and drink of the cup. For he who eats and drinks in an unworthy manner eats and drinks judgment to himself, not discerning the Lord's body (1 Corinthians 11:27-29).*

Some say that only those who are baptized with water can participate in the Holy Communion. But when we accept Jesus Christ, we receive the Holy Spirit as the gift. We all have the right to become the children of God.

Therefore, if we have received the Holy Spirit and become God's children, we can participate in the Holy Communion after repenting of our sins, even though we have not been baptized yet with water.

Through the Holy Communion, we once again remember the grace of the Lord who was hung on the cross and shed His blood for us. We should also look back on ourselves and learn and practice the word of God.

1 Corinthians 11:23-25 says, *"For I received from the Lord that which I also delivered to you, that the Lord Jesus in the night in which He was betrayed took bread; and when He had given thanks, He broke it and said, 'This is My body,*

which is for you; do this in remembrance of Me.' In the same way He took the cup also after supper, saying, 'This cup is the new covenant in My blood; do this, as often as you drink it, in remembrance of Me.'"

Therefore, I urge you to realize the true meaning of the Passover and the Holy Communion and diligently eat the flesh and drink the blood of the Lord so that you can cast off all forms of evil and accomplish circumcision of heart completely.

Chapter 9

Exodus and
the Feast of Unleavened Bread

Exodus 12:15-17

"Seven days you shall eat unleavened bread, but on the first day you shall remove leaven from your houses; for whoever eats anything leavened from the first day until the seventh day, that person shall be cut off from Israel. On the first day you shall have a holy assembly, and another holy assembly on the seventh day; no work at all shall be done on them, except what must be eaten by every person, that alone may be prepared by you. You shall also observe the Feast of Unleavened Bread, for on this very day I brought your hosts out of the land of Egypt; therefore you shall observe this day throughout your generations as a permanent ordinance".

"Let us forgive, but not forget."

It is a sentence written at the entrance of the Yad Vashem Holocaust Museum in Jerusalem. It is to keep in memory those six million Jews who were killed by the Nazis during the second World War, and not to repeat the same kind of history.

The history of Israel is a history of remembrances. In the Bible, God tells them to remember the past, bear it in mind, and keep it for generations.

After the Israelites were saved from the deaths of the firstborn by keeping the Passover and led out of Egypt, God told them to observe the Feast of Unleavened Bread. It is for them to eternally remember the day of being set free from slavery in Egypt.

Spiritual Meaning of Exodus

The day of the Exodus is not just a day of the freedom that the people of Israel recovered many thousands years ago.

The 'Egypt' in which Israelites lived in bondage symbolizes 'this world' which is under the control of the enemy devil and Satan. Just as the Israelites were persecuted and maltreated while being slaves in Egypt, people suffer from pains and sorrow brought by the enemy devil and Satan when they do not know about God.

As the Israelites witnessed the Ten Plagues that took place through Moses, they came to know God. They followed Moses out of Egypt to go into the Promised Land of Canaan, which God had promised to their ancestor Abraham.

This is same as today's people who used to live without knowing God, but came to accept Jesus Christ.

The Israelites coming out of Egypt, where they were slaves, is comparable to people coming out of their slavery to the enemy devil and Satan by accepting Jesus Christ and becoming God's children.

Also, the journey of the Israelites to the Canaan Land, where it is flowing with milk and honey, is no different from the believers who are making the journey of faith towards the kingdom of heaven.

The Canaan Land, Flowing with Milk and Honey

In the process of the Exodus, God did not guide the Israelites directly into the Canaan Land. They had to journey in the wilderness because there was a strong nation called Philistia on the shortest way to Canaan.

To pass that land, they had to wage a war against the strong Philistines. God knew that, if they did, those people who did not have faith would want to go back to Egypt.

In the same way, those who have just accepted Jesus Christ

are not given true faith immediately. So, if they face a test that is as great as the powerful nation of Philistia and the Philistines, they may not pass it and finally forsake faith.

That is why God says, *"No temptation has overtaken you except such as is common to man; but God is faithful, who will not allow you to be tempted beyond what you are able, but with the temptation will also make the way of escape, that you may be able to bear it"* (1 Corinthians 10:13).

Just as the Israelites marched in the wilderness until they reached the Canaan Land, even after we become children of God, there lays ahead of us the journey of faith until we reach the kingdom of heaven, the Canaan Land.

Even though the wilderness was tough those who had faith but did not go back to Egypt because they looked forward to seeing the freedom, peace, and abundance in the Canaan Land that they could not enjoy in Egypt. It is the same for us today.

Even though we sometimes have to march on a narrow and difficult way, we believe the beautiful glory of heavenly kingdom. So, we don't consider the race of faith difficult, but overcome everything with the help and power of God.

Finally, the people of Israel began the journey to the land of Canaan, the land flowing with milk and honey. They left behind the lands where they had lived for more than 400 years and began their march of faith under the leadership of Moses.

There were people who were taking the cattle. Others were loading the clothing, silver, and gold that they received from

Egyptians. Some were packing the unleavened dough while still others were taking care of the little children and the elderly. The vast array of the Israelites who were hurrying themselves to depart, was endless.

> *"Now the sons of Israel journeyed from Rameses to Succoth, about six hundred thousand men on foot, aside from children. A mixed multitude also went up with them, along with flocks and herds, a very large number of livestock. They baked the dough which they had brought out of Egypt into cakes of unleavened bread. For it had not become leavened, since they were driven out of Egypt and could not delay, nor had they prepared any provisions for themselves" (Exodus 12:37-39).*

This day their hearts were full of freedom, hope and salvation. To celebrate this day, God commanded them to observe the Feast of Unleavened Bread throughout all generations.

Feast of Unleavened Bread

Today, in Christianity, we celebrate Easter in the place of the Feast of Unleavened Bread. Easter is the feast celebrated to give thanks to God for giving the forgiveness of all our sins through the crucifixion of Jesus. Also, we celebrate this as the day when it became possible for us to come out of darkness and into the light by His resurrection.

The Feast of Unleavened Bread is one of the three major feasts of Israel. It is to commemorate the fact that they came out of Egypt by the hand of God. Beginning with the night of the Passover, they eat unleavened bread for seven days.

Even after he and the Egyptians had suffered so many plagues, the Pharaoh did not change his mind. Finally Egypt had to suffer the deaths of the firstborn and Pharaoh himself lost his first son. Pharaoh hurriedly called for Moses and Aaron and told them to leave Egypt immediately. So, they didn't have time to leaven the bread. That is the reason they had to eat the unleavened bread.

Also, God let them eat the unleavened bread so that they could remember the times of suffering and give thanks for being set free from slavery.

Passover is the feast that commemorates being saved from the deaths of the firstborn. They eat lamb, bitter herbs, and unleavened bread. The Feast of Unleavened Bread is to commemorate the fact that they ate unleavened bread for a week in the wilderness after they hurriedly came out of Egypt.

Today, the Israelis take the whole week off to observe the Passover including the Feast of the Unleavened Bread.

> *You shall not eat leavened bread with it; seven days you shall eat with it unleavened bread, the bread of affliction (for you came out of the land of Egypt in haste), so that you may remember all the days of your*

> life the day when you came out of the land of Egypt (Deuteronomy 16:3).

Spiritual Meaning of Feast of Unleavened Bread

> Seven days you shall eat unleavened bread, but on the first day you shall remove leaven from your houses; for whoever eats anything leavened from the first day until the seventh day, that person shall be cut off from Israel (Exodus 12:15).

Here, the 'first day' refers to the day of salvation. After they were saved from the deaths of the firstborn and came out of Egypt, the Israelites had to eat unleavened bread for seven days. In the same way, after we accept Jesus Christ and receive the Holy Spirit, we have to spiritually eat unleavened bread to reach complete salvation.

Spiritually eating unleavened bread means to forsake the world and take the narrow way. After we accept Jesus Christ, we have to lower ourselves and go the narrow way to reach complete salvation with humble hearts.

To eat leavened bread instead of unleavened bread, is to take the wide and easy way in pursuit of the meaningless things of this world as one sees fit. Obviously, the person who takes this way will not receive salvation. That is why God said those who eat leavened bread would be cut off from Israel.

Then, what are the lessons that the Feast of Unleavened Bread is giving to us today?

First, we have to always remember and give thanks for the love of God and the grace of salvation that we freely receive in the redemption of Jesus Christ.

The Israelites remember the times of slavery in Egypt by eating the unleavened bread for seven days and give thanks to God for saving them. Likewise, we believers, who are the spiritual Israelites, must remember the grace and love of God who has guided us to the way of eternal life and give thanks in all things.

We have to remember the day when we met and experienced God and the day when we were born again with water and the Spirit and to give thanks to God in remembrance of His grace. This is the same as observing a spiritual level of the Feast of Unleavened Bread. Those who are truly good in heart will never forget any of the grace they have received from the Lord. This is the duty of man and this is the action of the beautiful heart of goodness.

With this good heart, no matter how difficult the present reality is, we will never forget the love and grace but give thanks for His grace and rejoice always.

It was the case with Habakkuk, who was active during the reign of King Josiah around 600 BC.

> *Though the fig tree should not blossom And there be no fruit on the vines, Though the yield of the olive should fail And the fields produce no food, Though the flock should be cut off from the fold And there be no cattle in the stalls, Yet I will exult in the LORD, I will rejoice in the God of my salvation (Habakkuk 3:17-18).*

His country Judah had to face the dangers from the Chaldeans (Babylonians), and Prophet Habakkuk had to see his country going to fall, but rather than falling into despair, Habakkuk offered up praises of thanks to God.

Likewise, regardless of our situation or condition in life, with just the one fact that we are saved by God's grace without any cost, we can be thankful from the bottom of our hearts.

Second, we should not habitually continue our lives of faith nor backslide to a former dry way of life nor lead a Christian life that has no progression or change.

Following an unenthusiastic life as a Christian is to stay as we were. It is a stagnant life without movement or change. It means that we have lukewarm, habitual faith. It is showing the formalities of faith, without circumcising our hearts.

If we are cold, we may receive some kind of punishment from God so that we can change and be renewed. But if we are lukewarm, we compromise with the world and do not try to cast off sins. We will not consciously and easily leave God completely because we have received the Holy Spirit and we know very well that there is heaven and hell.

If we feel our shortcomings, we will pray to God about them. But those who are lukewarm do not show any enthusiasm. They become 'churchgoers'.

They may have afflictions and feel the anguish and anxiety in their hearts, but as time passes, even these feelings disappear.

"So because you are lukewarm, and neither hot nor cold, I will spit you out of My mouth" (Revelation 3:16). As said, then, they cannot be saved. That is why God makes us observe different feasts from time to time to check our faith and to reach a fully grown up and mature measure of faith.

Third, we always have to keep the grace of the first love. If we have lost it, we have to think about that point where we have fallen, repent, and quickly recover the first deeds.

Anyone who has accepted the Lord Jesus can experience the grace of the first love. The grace and love of God is so great that each day of his life will be joy and happiness itself.

Just as parents expect their children to grow up, God also expects His children to have firmer faith and reach greater measures of faith. But if we lose the grace of the first love at one point, our enthusiasm and love may cool down. Even if we pray, we may just do it with only a sense of duty.

Until we reach a whole, complete and full level of sanctification, if we give over our heart to Satan, we may lose the first love any time. Thus, if we have lost the grace of the fervent first love, we have to find the reason and quickly repent and turn back.

Many people say that a Christian life is a narrow and difficult way, but Deuteronomy 30:11 says, *"For this commandment which I command you today is not too difficult for you, nor is it out of reach."* If we realize the true love of God, the journey of life in faith is never difficult. It is because the present sufferings cannot be compared with the glory that will be given to us later. We can be happy to imagine that glory.

Therefore, as believers who are living during the last days, we should always obey the word of God and live in light all the time. If we do not take the wide way of the world but instead the narrow way of faith, we will be able to enter into the Canaan Land flowing with milk and honey.

God will give us the grace of salvation and joy of the first love. He will bless us to accomplish sanctification and through our march of faith, He will allow us to take the eternal heavenly kingdom by force.

Chapter 10

Life of Obedience and Blessings

Deuteronomy 28:1-14

Now it shall be, if you diligently obey the LORD your God, being careful to do all His commandments which I command you today, the LORD your God will set you high above all the nations of the earth. All these blessings will come upon you and overtake you if you obey the LORD your God: Blessed shall you be in the city, and blessed shall you be in the country. Blessed shall be the offspring of your body and the produce of your ground and the offspring of your beasts, the increase of your herd and the young of your flock. Blessed shall be your basket and your kneading bowl. Blessed shall you be when you come in, and blessed shall you be when you go out.

The history of Israel's Exodus gives us valuable lessons. Just as plagues came upon Pharaoh and Egypt for their disobedience, on the way to the Land of Canaan the people of Israel had to suffer trials and failed to have prosperity because they went against will of God.

They were spared from the plague of death of the firstborn through the Passover. But, when they didn't have water to drink and food to eat on their way to Canaan, they began to complain.

They made a golden calf and worshipped it, and gave bad reports about the Promised Land; they even stood against Moses. All was because they did not look at the way to Canaan with the eyes of faith.

As a result, the first generation of the Exodus, except Joshua and Caleb, all died in the wilderness. Only Joshua and Caleb believed the promise of God and obeyed Him, and they entered into the Canaan Land with the second generation of the Exodus.

The Blessing of Entering into Canaan Land

Since the first generation of Exodus were part of the generations that were born and raised in the Gentile culture of Egypt for 400 years, they had lost much of their faith in God. Also, a great deal of evil was planted into their hearts while they went through persecutions and sufferings.

But the Israelites of the second generation of the Exodus

were taught the word of God since they were young. Because they witnessed many powerful works of God, they were very different from their parents' generation.

They understood why their parents' generation could not go into the Canaan Land but had to stay in the wilderness for forty years. They were fully ready to obey God and their leader with true faith.

Unlike their parents' generation who continually complained even after experiencing numerous works of God, they vowed to obey fully. They confessed that they would completely obey Joshua who succeeded Moses by the will of God.

> *Just as we obeyed Moses in all things, so we will obey you; only may the LORD your God be with you as He was with Moses. Anyone who rebels against your command and does not obey your words in all that you command him, shall be put to death; only be strong and courageous (Joshua 1:17-18).*

The forty years in the wilderness during which the Israelites wandered about, was not just a time of punishment. It was a time of spiritual training for the second generation of Exodus who would enter into the land of Canaan.

Before God gives blessings to us, He permits many different kinds of spiritual trainings so that we can have spiritual faith. It's because without spiritual faith, we cannot receive salvation and we cannot go into heavenly kingdom.

Also, if God gives us blessings before we have spiritual faith, it is likely that most of us would go back to the world. So, God shows us amazing works of His power, and sometimes allows us fiery trials so that our faith can grow.

The first hurdle of obedience that the second generation faced was at the Jordan River. The Jordan River ran between the plains of Moab and the Canaan Land, and at that time, the flow was strong and often flooded its banks.

Here, what did God say? He told the priests to carry the Ark of Covenant and to march in the lead to be the first to step into the river. As soon as the people heard the will of God through Joshua, they marched towards the Jordan River without hesitation, with the priests in front.

Because they believed in the all-knowing and all-powerful God, they could obey without any doubt or complaints. As a result, when the feet of the priests carrying the Ark touched the water at the river's edge, the flow of water stopped and they could cross it like dry land.

Also, they destroyed the city of Jericho that was said to be an impregnable fortress. Unlike today, as they didn't have powerful weapons, it was almost impossible to destroy such strong walls, which were actually two layers of walls.

Even with all their strength, it would have been a tremendously difficult task to destroy it. But God told them to just march around the city once a day for six days, and on the seventh day, to rise early and march around it seven times, and then shout with loud voice.

In a situation where the enemy forces stood guard on top of the walls, the second generation of the Exodus began to march around the city walls without hesitation.

It was possible that their enemy could have shot so many arrows against them or they could have launched full scale attack against them. Still in that dangerous situation they obeyed with word of God and just marched around the city. Even the strong walls had to collapse when the people of Israel obeyed the word of God.

To Receive Blessings through Obedience

Obedience can transcend any kind of circumstances. It is the passageway to bring down the amazing power of God. From a human perspective, we may think that it is impossible to obey a certain thing. But in God's sight, there is nothing that we cannot obey, and God is almighty.

To show this kind of obedience, just as we have to roast the lamb over the fire, we have to hear and understand the word of God fully by the inspiration of the Holy Spirit.

Also, just as the people of Israel have observed the Passover and the Feast of Unleavened Bread throughout the generations, we always have to remember the word of God and keep it in our mind. Namely, we have to continually circumcise our heart with the word of God and cast off sins and evil with our gratitude for the grace of salvation.

Only then will we be given true faith and show the perfect deed of obedience.

There may be things that we cannot obey if we think with the theories, knowledge, or common sense of man. But the will of God for us is to still obey even in these things. When we show this kind of obedience, God shows us great works and wondrous blessings.

In the Bible, many people received incredible blessings through their obedience. Daniel and Joseph received blessings because they had firm faith in God, and even before death, they only kept the word of God. Also through the life of Abraham, the Father of Faith, we can understand how pleased God is with those who obey.

The Blessings Given to Abraham

Now the LORD said to Abram, "Go forth from your country, and from your relatives and from your father's house, to the land which I will show you; and I will make you a great nation, and I will bless you, and make your name great; and so you shall be a blessing" (Genesis 12:1-2).

At that time, Abraham was seventy-five, he was definitely not young. Especially, it wasn't easy for him to leave his country and depart from all his relatives since he didn't have any sons to be his heirs.

God didn't designate any place to go, either. God just commanded him to leave. If human thought was utilized, it was very difficult to obey. He had to leave behind everything that he had accumulated there, and go to a completely foreign place.

It is not easy to leave everything we have and go to a completely new place, even if there is a sure guarantee about the future. And how many people can actually leave everything he has now, when their future is not so clear? But Abraham just obeyed.

There was another occasion where Abraham's obedience shone its light more brightly. To receive Abraham's obedience more perfectly, God allowed him a test to give him blessings.

Namely, God commanded him to offer his only son Isaac. Isaac was such a precious son to Abraham. He was even more valuable than he himself was, but he obeyed without any hesitation.

After God spoke to him, we find in Genesis 22:3 that very next day, he rose early in the morning and prepared things to give a sacrifice to God, and went to the place of which God had told him.

This time, it was a higher level of obedience than the one to leave his country and his father's house. At that time, he just obeyed without really knowing the will of God. But when God told him to offer his son Isaac as a burnt offering, he understood God's heart and obeyed His will. In Hebrews 11:17-19 it is recorded how he believed that even if he were to offer his son as a burnt offering, God would revive him, for he was the seed of the promised of God.

God was delighted with this faith of Abraham and He himself prepared the sacrifice. After Abraham passed this test, God called him His friend and gave him great blessings.

Even today, water is scarce around Israel. It was even more scarce at that time in Canaan Land. But wherever Abraham went, there was abundance in water. And even his nephew Lot, who was staying with him, received such a great blessing.

Abraham had many cattle, and much silver, and gold; he was very rich. When his nephew Lot was taken as a captive, Abraham took 318 men who were raised in his house, and rescued Lot. Just by seeing this fact, we can see how rich he was.

Abraham obeyed the word of God. The land and the vicinity around him together received blessings, and those who were with him also received blessings.

Through Abraham, his son Isaac received blessings, too, and his descendants were so many that they came to form even a nation. Furthermore, God told him that God would bless whoever blessed him, and He would curse whoever cursed him. He was so respected that even the kings of the neighboring nations paid tribute to him.

Abraham received all kinds of blessings that one can receive on this earth, including wealth, fame, authority, health, and children. Just as written in chapter 28 of Deuteronomy, he received blessings when he came in and when he went out.

He became the source of blessings and the father of faith. Moreover, he could deeply understand the heart of God and God could share His heart with him as His friend. How glorious blessing this is!

Because God is love, He wants everyone to become like Abraham and reach the blessed and glorious positions. That is why God left detailed record about Abraham. Whoever follows his example and obeys the word of God can receive the same blessings when he comes in and when he goes out as Abraham did.

The Love and Justice of God Who Wants to Bless Us

Until now we looked into the Ten Plagues inflicted upon Egypt and the Passover which was the way of salvation for the Israelites. Through this we can understand why we face disasters, how we can avoid them, and how we can be saved.

If we are suffering from problems or diseases, we have to realize that it is originally caused by our evils. Then, we have to quickly look back on ourselves, repent, and cast off all forms of evil. Also, through Abraham, we can understand what kinds of wondrous and unimaginable blessings God gives to those who obey Him.

There are causes for all disasters. According to how much we realize them with heart, turn away from sin and evil, and change ourselves, the results will be very different. Some people will just pay the penalty of their wrongdoings, while some others will find the darkness or evil in their heart through the suffering and make it a chance to change themselves.

In Deuteronomy chapter 28, we can find the comparisons of the blessings and curses that will come upon us in situations of obedience and disobedience to the word of God.

God wants to give us blessings, but as He said in Deuteronomy 11:26, *"See, I am setting before you today a blessing and a curse,"* the choice is up to us. If we sow beans, beans will sprout. Likewise, we suffer disasters brought by Satan as a result of our sins. In this case, God has to allow the disasters to occur to us according to His justice.

Parents want their children to be well-off, and they say, "Study hard," "Live an upright life," "Obey all the traffic regulations" and so forth. With this same kind of heart, God has given us His commandments and He wants us to obey them. Parents would never want their children to disobey them and fall into ways of misfortune and destruction. Likewise, it is never the will of God for us to suffer from troubles.

Therefore, I pray in the name of the Lord Jesus Christ that you will all realize that the will of God for His children is not disaster but blessing and through the life of obedience, you will receive blessings when you come in and when you go out, and everything will go well with you.

The Author
Dr. Jaerock Lee

Dr. Jaerock Lee was born in Muan, Jeonnam Province, Republic of Korea, in 1943. In his twenties, he suffered from a variety of incurable diseases for seven years and awaited death with no hope for recovery. One day in the spring of 1974, however, he was led to a church by his sister, and when he knelt down to pray, the living God immediately healed him of all his diseases.

From the moment Dr. Lee met the living God through that wonderful experience, he has loved God with all his heart and sincerity, and in 1978 was called to be a servant of God. He prayed fervently so that he could clearly understand the will of God and wholly accomplish it, and obeyed all the word of God. In 1982, he founded Manmin Church in Seoul, S. Korea, and countless works of God, including miraculous healings and wonders, have been taking place at his church.

In 1986, Dr. Lee was ordained as a pastor at the Annual Assembly of Jesus' Sungkyul Church of Korea, and four years later in 1990, his sermons began to be broadcast on the Far East Broadcasting Company, the Asia Broadcast Station, and the Washington Christian Radio System to Australia, Russia, the Philippines, and many more.

Three years later in 1993, Manmin Central Church was selected as one of the "World's Top 50 Churches" by the *Christian World* magazine (US) and he received an Honorary Doctorate of Divinity from Christian Faith College, Florida, USA, and in 1996 a Ph. D. in Ministry from Kingsway Theological Seminary, Iowa, USA.

Since 1993, Dr. Lee has taken the lead in world mission through many overseas crusades in L.A., New York, Baltimore, Hawaii of the USA, Tanzania, Argentina, Uganda, Japan, Pakistan, Kenya, the Philippines,

Honduras, India, Russia, Germany, Peru, and Democratic Republic of Congo, and in 2002 he was called a "worldwide pastor" by major Christian newspapers in Korea for his work in various overseas crusades.

As of August 2009, Manmin Central Church is a congregation of more than 100,000 members and has 9,000 branch churches throughout the globe including 52 domestic branch churches in major cities, and has so far commissioned more than 133 missionaries to 25 countries, including the United States, Russia, Germany, Canada, Japan, China, France, India, Kenya, and many more.

To this day, Dr. Lee has written 57 books, including bestsellers *Tasting Eternal Life before Death*, *My Life My Faith I & II*, *The Way of Salvation*, *The Measure of Faith*, *Heaven I & II*, and *Hell*, and his works have been being translated into more than 41 languages.

His Christian columns appear on *The Hankook Ilbo*, *The JoongAng Daily*, *The Dong-A Ilbo*, *The Munhwa Ilbo*, *The Seoul Shinmun*, *The Kyunghyang Shinmun*, *The Hankyoreh Shinmun*, *The Korea Economic Daily*, *The Korea Herald*, *The Shisa News*, *The Christian Press* and *The Nation Evangelization Newspaper*.

Dr. Lee is currently leader of many missionary organizations and associations including: Chairman, The United Holiness Church of Jesus Christ; Permanent President of the World Christianity Revival Mission Association; President, The Nation Evangelization Newspaper; President, Manmin World Mission; Founder, Manmin TV; Founder & Board Chairman, Global Christian Network (GCN); Founder & Board Chairman, World Christian Doctors Network (WCDN); and Founder & Board Chairman, Manmin International Seminary (MIS).

Other powerful books by the same author

Heaven I & II

A detailed sketch of the gorgeous living environment the heavenly citizens enjoy and beautiful description of different levels of heavenly kingdoms.

The Message of the Cross

A powerful awakening message for all the people who are spiritually asleep In this book you will find the reason Jesus is the only Savior and the true love of God.

Hell

An earnest message to all mankind from God, who wishes not even one soul to fall into the depths of hell! You will discover the never-before-revealed account of the cruel reality of the Lower Grave and hell.

Tasting Eternal Life Before Death

A testimonial memoirs of Dr. Jaerock Lee, who was born gain and saved from the valley of death and has been leading an exemplary Christian life.

The Measure of Faith

What kind of a dwelling place, crown and reward are prepared for you in heaven? This book provides with wisdom and guidance for you to measure your faith and cultivate the best and most mature faith.

www.urimbooks.com

www.ingramcontent.com/pod-product-compliance
Lightning Source LLC
LaVergne TN
LVHW010329070526
838199LV00065B/5704